WRITE SOURCE 2000

A Guide to
Writing, Thinking,
& Learning

Teacher's Guide

A Teacher's Guide to accompany

Write Source 2000

D0897438

To Middle-School Educators

If you are committed to middle-school education, you are a very special person. It is for you and your students that we have designed our *Write Source 2000* handbook and supporting materials.

This guidebook will not only help you use our handbook effectively and wisely, but it will also help you review your roots as a teacher. We have tried to address many of the "big questions" teachers are asking today in such a way that this guidebook will help you integrate your professional experience with current research.

If you have any questions, please call. (Use our toll-free number—1-800-428-8071.) We are always ready to help you or receive your feedback.

The Write Source/D.C. Heath

Published simultaneously in Canada

Printed in the United States of America

International Standard Book Number: 0-669-40143-9

1 2 3 4 5 6 7 8 9 10 -HLG- 00 99 98 97 96 95

What You'll Find Inside

Write Source 2000 Student Handbook— Guiding Principles

As we developed *Write Source 2000,* the following principles served as our guide:

- **CHARMING** A handbook must have **character and a special charm.** It has to have the look and feel of a fun book—one that students can open up and see something they like, something pleasing to their eye, something that will get them to read the information on the page.

- **HELPFUL** Students must know that any chunk of information in a handbook will help them in some way. It must get them to say, **"So that is how you ...."** It must help them make sense out of their writing and learning and point them in the right direction to continue their work.

- **STIMULATING** Students should feel aesthetically satisfied each time they open a handbook. They should also feel intellectually stimulated by the way information is presented. And they should feel generally reassured that each time they open a handbook, they will have a guiding and understanding hand **pointing them in the right direction**.

- **CONCISE** We know that students aren't going to keep coming back to a handbook if they have to read large chunks of copy to get the information they're after, so there has to be a **get-to-the-point quality** to the book. It has to look good and it has to make a difference. Students have to feel that their handbook was written for them, that it speaks to them, that it is their personal teacher's aide.

- **SEQUENTIAL** A handbook must essentially be a "how-to" book. Students have to feel confident that when they open a handbook, it tells them what they can or should do first, second, third, and so on. It must supply all of the basic rules, definitions, explanations, and principles they need. And the information should be presented with reassurance—**a hand-on-the-shoulder quality**.

- **INVOLVING** A handbook should be a "how-to" book in another sense: It should get students interested, engaged, and moving forward in their writing and learning. It should be thought of as **a process book** much more than a product book. Getting students started and keeping their learning going are just as important as advising them how to wrap up their writing and learning.

- **CONVERSATIONAL** A handbook should make students curious, active, and engaged in learning each time they open it up. And it must keep the learning dialogue going as long as possible.

- **INVITING** Alfred North Whitehead calls early adolescence the years of romance in education—a time to explore and experiment; a time when precision plays second fiddle to taking risks, experimenting, and exploring. A handbook should reflect this. A handbook should be **an invitation to learning**.

- **TIMELY** A handbook should reflect the latest and the best research on writing, thinking, and learning. It should provide students with effective writing-to-learn and prewriting ideas, with insights into cooperative learning, and with the latest in reading and study techniques. A contemporary handbook should also include whatever else is new and important in learning for today's students.

Does the final product live up to these principles? Absolutely. But don't take our word for it. Open your copy of *Write Source 2000* and see for yourself.

A Quick Tour

The following pages contain a brief

but informative look at the *Write*

Source 2000 handbook and how it can

work for you and your students.

Write Source 2000
A Quick Tour

Write Source 2000 serves as the perfect handbook for students and teachers in the middle grades and beyond, one which will help your students improve their ability *to write* (prewriting through proofreading), *to think* (creatively, logically, and clearly), and *to learn* (in the classroom, in small groups, and independently). This guided tour will highlight its major points of interest and learning.

Introductory copy previews the contents of each chapter and stimulates students to read on. Students will appreciate that each page is a complete text unto itself, beginning with an identifying title or subtitle and ending at a natural stopping point in the text.

The quotations which appear throughout *Write Source 2000* provide food for thought and discussion for you and your students.

003

Writing to Learn

Each section begins with a division page which includes a mini table of contents plus a stimulating full-color illustration. The numbers refer to topic numbers, not page numbers.

The titles for many of the sections reflect our belief in an integrated approach to language learning. In addition to "Writing to Learn" there are sections entitled "Searching to Learn," "Thinking to Learn," "Speaking and Listening to Learn," and "Learning to Learn."

006-007

Writing to Learn

Don't be puzzled by the title. We don't have it backwards. Writing to learn is just what we mean. But I can understand why you might be confused. You are, after all, in school to learn to write with the help of your teachers, your classmates, and our handbook. So what gives? Why did we call this section "Writing to Learn"? Read on and find out.

006

If you've read the previous page, you already know why "Writing to Learn" is a good title for this chapter. It is by writing that you learn to write. You can read about writing and you can talk about it until you're blue in the face, but unless you practice writing, you really can't expect to make any major improvements. That doesn't mean that reading and talking about writing aren't important, because they are. But they only make a difference if you regularly put pen to paper.

Anybody who becomes good at something that requires a certain amount of skill does so through practice. How do you think Michael Jordan became such a good basketball player? Did he do it by watching basketball games, by playing HORSE, by talking a good game? Of course he didn't. He practiced for hours on end, and I'm sure he still does.

(By the way, unless you think otherwise, writers aren't born with a special writing gene or blessed by the writing fairy. Some seem to come by the ability to write more easily than others, but it is still a skill that we must all practice.)

007 **Writing Leads to Active Learning**

There's another reason for the title. Writing can help you learn more effectively in any field or area, be it language arts or industrial arts, social studies or science. I know. It might sound like we're venturing a bit out of our orbit here and making too much out of writing. But let me just share a few ideas with you.

We all agree that to become good at something, you have to roll up your sleeves and get actively involved, right? And this is exactly what you should do to become good at learning. Most of you are already involved, for the most part. You listen in class and take notes. You read what's required of you, complete homework assignments, and study for tests.

"I hear and I forget; I see and I remember; I write and I understand."
Chinese Proverb

The helpful checklists in *Write Source 2000* provide students with efficient and effective pointers as they develop their writing and learning.

The Writing Process 026-027

Correcting: *Preparing the Final Copy* 026

There will come a point in each writing assignment when you'll be satisfied that you've made all of the necessary changes (or your due date is fast approaching). This is the time to get your writing ready to share. During this final step you should first check for missing words. You should also check for spelling, mechanics, usage, and grammatical errors. Then it is time to prepare a neat final draft and proofread it.

Correcting and Proofreading Checklist 027

The following guidelines will help you put the finishing touches on your writing:

Spelling (See 563.)
- Have you spelled all of the words correctly? (Read your writing backwards one word at a time when you check for spelling. Then you can't help but focus on each word and check it for spelling.)

Punctuation (See 458.)
- Does each sentence end with an end punctuation mark?
- Have you placed commas before the conjunctions *and, but,* or *or* in compound sentences? Have you used commas to set off items listed in a series?
- Are apostrophes in place to show possession or to mark contractions?
- Have you properly punctuated any dialogue or written conversation with quotation marks?

Capitalization (See 533.)
- Have you started sentences and dialogue with a capital letter?
- Have you capitalized specific names of people, places, or things?

Usage (See 574.)
- Have you misused any of the commonly mixed pairs of words: *there, their, they're; to, too, two; its, it's; are, our; your, you're.*

Grammar (See 695 and 090-114.)
- Do your subjects and verbs agree?
- Do your pronouns agree with their antecedents?
- Have you unintentionally used any sentence fragments or rambling or run-on sentences?

117

117 Writing That's in Style

Read the parts of three stories which follow. The natural writing voice of the writer comes through in each selection.

> After that, I was underwater in a silent world, all alone. It was great. But my air was running out and I had to surface. I gave out a kick with my left leg; then two or three more and I surfaced. I dog-paddled to the side of the pool, paused, then lifted myself to the side. I was exhausted.

> While we were walking, I looked up and saw the moon was out. It made the fog seem to glow. Off in the distance, I heard a dog bark and then a chorus of barks. I felt a shiver crawl up my spine, probably just the cold.

> "I've thought it over. I'm not going on the Eagle."
> "But it'll be fun. C'mon!"
> "No! I just ate lunch. I'm not going on it."
> "Oh, gees! It's not that bad. You're not going to puke."
> "I know it, but I don't like going upside down."
> "Yes you do."
> "No I don't."
> "I'll give you a dollar."
> "Okay."
> We got into the last car of the roller coaster and locked ourselves in. We started to move and slowly submerged into the Eagle's tunnel. I felt like I was the camera on one of those <u>National Geographic</u> specials going into some creature's mouth and down its throat.

These selections make us pay attention to what is being said because each seems so real and so natural. And we can tell that each student writer is interested in telling a good story. In the first example, it is easy to visualize the writer kicking to the surface of the water. In the second example, we can share the writer's feeling of uneasiness while walking late at night. In the last humorous example, we can share the writer's fear and uncertainty of a roller coaster called the Eagle.

 MINI-lesson

Writing voices are something like clothing styles. There is a different style for different occasions. You use a natural voice when you want to share information, a goofy mixture of voices when you're going for laughs, and somebody else's voice when you're trying to borrow a little bit of his or her attitude.

The many minilessons provide you and your students with added insights and enrichment activities.

A helpful student or professional model complements each set of writing guidelines. The models are annotated so students can best understand and appreciate them.

Writing Phase Autobiographies 141

Model Short Phase Autobiography 141

In the sample phase autobiography which follows, the student author remembers a time in her life when she enjoyed dreaming up and pretending to be someone else. In fact, she did it so often that it became something she was "notorious for." This dress-up time in her life is considered a "phase," a period of time when a person does something day after day, week after week, sometimes month after month. Read the model and take note of the comments.

Fashionation

The writer begins with a clear, yet creative way of introducing her topic.

When I was younger, I was notorious for my strange dress-up games. One of these games was "Keeku." When I played Keeku, I would pin my hair up with plastic barrettes and hold a pair of red sunglass frames that only had one handle. With my costume complete, I would run around the house saying "Keeku! Keeku! Keeku!" It wasn't much of a game, but I guess I enjoyed it because I did it all the time.

The writer supplies plenty of details so the reader can get a clear picture of what she looked like.

I also spent a lot of time playing "Ginger." The main thing I needed to play this was my "Ginger dress" or squiggly skirt as it was sometimes called. It was a multi-colored tank top nobody wore anymore, and it was like a dress on me. I would put it on, tie a belt around it, and an amazing change would take place. I was no longer Lisa; instead, I was beautiful, glamorous Ginger from *Gilligan's Island*. I'd walk around the house calling my sisters and brothers Mary Ann, Gilligan, Skipper, or Mr. and Mrs. Howell. The title Professor was reserved for the St. Agnes statue in our living room which was just my size.

The student writer recalls a specific incident which adds to the overall picture we have of her.

Once when I was playing "Ginger," I added something new to the game; it was my Ginger hairstyle. This delicate design was created by sucking my hair up into the vacuum cleaner hose until it stood on end. I thought I was pretty beautiful until the neighbor boys began teasing me about it. I gave up my Ginger hairdo.

My days of make-believe sometimes included my sister Mary, who was my constant companion. We played long dresses or dressed up in our ballerina dresses. Hers was blue and mine was pink. They itched worse than poison ivy, but we'd wear them for hours. We wore them when we played house and store and restaurant . . . and even when we rode our Big Wheels down the driveway.

The writer concludes that everyone has a similar experience.

I guess all kids go through a pretending stage. Why dressing up was so important to me, though, I don't know. Today I wouldn't be caught dead looking like that.

Writing Phase Biographies   151-152

Writing Phase Biographies

I wish I had a hand-held 3-D Supersensory Biographical Single-Phase Translator. Then with a few twists of a knob I could tune in a picture of an interesting phase of someone else's life.

For example, I'd like to know

■ when and why Abraham Lincoln decided to run for president,

■ what life was like for my oldest living relative when he or she was my age, and

■ all about an important period of change in the life of the most fascinating person I know.

Fortunately, I don't have to wait until A.D. 2001 for a 3-D SBSPT. You can invent one for me now by writing a "Phase Biography." But don't stop there. This section offers you encouragement and helpful guidelines to continue inventing.

What Is a Phase Biography?   151

A "phase bio" is a short, truthful story about an interesting or important period of somebody's life. It's something like the phase autobiography, 133, except it's focused on somebody besides you. And memory won't be enough. You will need to do some poking around: maybe researching in books and magazines, maybe interviewing a person or others who knew that person, maybe tape-recording the interview. All that extra legwork will reward you with new insights and will make your biography one that you and your reader will appreciate.

Getting It Started   152

Look around. Your best subject might be very close at hand. Consider people in your life: friends at school, acquaintances of your parents, relatives. Some subjects may be more distant: ancestors, historical figures, famous people. You need to have a "nose" for interesting stories.

R.J. chose a friend of the family as the subject of his phase biography. His name is Armand and he's one of the best oil painters in the state of Michigan. More importantly, he is wise, powerful, and in love with nature in its unspoiled condition. He is more magnetic than anyone R.J. has ever met.

Writing Dialogue   255-256

Guidelines for Developing Dialogue   255

To develop good dialogues you do not have to follow any absolute rules. But here are some guidelines that may help you shape the conversations in your stories:

※ Use words which your characters would actually use if they were able to speak. (Remember that people express what they have to say in different ways.)

※ Get rid of any dialogue that just kills time. (There should always be a purpose for the dialogue—to reveal character, to set up a surprise, to intensify the action, or to lead toward a resolution.)

※ Most of the dialogue should be about the speaker's beliefs or problems. (Generally one speaker's beliefs clash with another's. This adds drama to the story.)

※ Write the dialogue as speakers actually speak. (People often interrupt each other in conversation, and, at other times, talk past or ignore each other.)

※ Stop the conversation at the right spot. (The characters don't have to say everything. Leave some things to the reader's imagination.)

※ Write and punctuate the dialogue so it is easy to read. (Indent every time someone new speaks and identify the speaker if it isn't clear who is talking. See "The Yellow Pages" for help punctuating.)

A Sample Dialogue

A portion of dialogue from a student narrative follows. Note how the conversation intensifies the action.

256

Junior and I entered a dark and dreary room at the end of the tunnel. It was full of cobwebs, old crates, and debris scattered all over the place. I could faintly hear water dripping.

After a few uneasy minutes, I said, "I think we better get out of here."

"Come on. Nothing is going to happen," Junior replied.

"I don't care. This place gives me the creeps!"

"All right, let's go."

As we were making our way out, Junior bumped into one of the supporting beams.

"We've got to move faster, Junior! I think this place might cave in!"

"I'm right behind you!"

Just as we reached the tunnel opening, the old place collapsed. There were rocks, mud, and splintered wood everywhere. Junior and I just looked at each other, knowing that if we had remained in that room just a few seconds longer, we would have been goners.

Students are provided with a "catalog" of writing forms—progressing from very personal forms of writing to more public forms. The entertaining and helpful copy in all sections of *Write Source 2000* speaks to young learners.

153

158   **Biography Sampler**

The feature editor is a gruff-looking veteran of the newspaper business. You enter his office for your first assignment. He looks up and says, "We need some stories about real people, interesting people, for our Sunday magazine. Get out there and see what you can come up with." That's it—no other guidelines or helpful hints. But don't worry. We've got you covered with the bio-writing forms described below. So go out there and see what you can find.

Oral History: Do you know an old woman with strong hands and a joyful, wise twinkle in her eye? Do you want to know how she got her twinkle? Ask her. Bring a tape recorder if she says that's okay. Have more questions to ask her, but let her tell you what she wants. Read about different periods she has lived through. Use your reading to help you give your interview shape when you write it up.

Bio-Poem: Here's a challenge: squeeze somebody's life into 11 fascinating lines. Make the first line the first name, the last line the last name. In between, make your character live and breathe. Here's one scheme: line 1, *First name;* line 2, *One key adjective*; line 3, *Brother (or sister) of (fill in)*; line 4, *Lover of (name three things)*; line 5, *Who feels (three things)*; line 6, *Who needs (three things)*; line 7, *Who gives (three things)*; line 8, *Who fears (three things)*; line 9, *Who would like to see (three things)*; line 10, *Resident of (what city?)*; line 11, *Last name.* But why use my idea? Whip up your own.

Chronicle: Write a story for your local newspaper about what some notable person did, either recently or far back in history. For example, maybe a local musician has recently joined a well-known rock band. Interview someone who knows him or her. Read about the person. Then choose an interesting angle and write a story which is both informative and entertaining.

▲ For each basic writing form, students are provided with a sampler of related writing ideas.

Students are provided with clear and concise writing guidelines for each basic form of writing discussed in *Write Source 2000*.

A thought-provoking and creative scenario appropriately introduces the in-depth discussion of the thinking process.

Thinking Better 306

Thinking Better

Would you like to be a faster thinker . . . more logical or creative? How about learning to keep more thoughts in mind and holding them in focus? Would you like to clear up your muddy thinking? Would you like to think longer and harder? How about some step-by-step help through some hard problems? Would you like to do better in school? Read on.

The Planet of Bad Thinkers
306

Suppose you're an astronaut and your space capsule accidentally slips out of orbit. You sail through the blackness of space and finally land on a planet called BLOK. While NASA sends out a rescue ship, you decide to look around. What you discover is astounding. The creatures on BLOK, who call themselves Chips, are *bad thinkers*. Every one of them. Everything they try fails. Everything they build falls down. It's a miracle they survive. They don't seem to understand anything.

You don't know if NASA will ever find you, but in case they ever do, you make a list of all the things the Chips do wrong when they try to think. Someday your list might save your fellow Earthlings from making a mess of their own planet.

What would you put on your list? Maybe something like this:

Why the Chips Are Down

1. Chips are in too big a hurry.
2. They never set goals.
3. They never ask questions.
4. They ignore the evidence.
5. They believe whatever they read.
6. They go with the crowd.
7. They stick with their first emotional reaction; they also talk in cliches and think in slogans.
8. They never connect what they've learned in one subject to another.
9. They never think about *how* they think.
10. They never write anything down.

▓ Is it any wonder the planet BLOK is a mess? If you ever get home to Earth, don't be a Chip off the old BLOK. And warn your fellow Earthlings what can happen if they turn into bad thinkers.

Thinking Logically 343

Thinking Logically

When you want to make (or prove) an important point in either speaking or writing, you must "connect" your ideas in just the right way—in a clear, logical way. The suggestions which follow will help you make these connections.

For your thinking to be logical, it has to make sense. It has to "hold up" under careful examination by your audience. It has to be **reasonable** (supported with good reasons) and **reliable** (supported with solid evidence). In short, your thinking has to be believable.

So how do you go about making your thinking believable and, therefore, acceptable to your audience? Generally speaking, you must organize, support, and present your points *so well* that your audience cannot disagree with or question what you've said or written. Specifically, you can follow the process or stages listed below. (These steps are especially useful when putting together debates, speeches, research papers, etc.)

Becoming a Logical Thinker
343

▓ **Decide** on your purpose and state it clearly on the top of your paper.

▓ **Gather** whatever information you can on the topic.

▓ **Focus** on a central "claim" or point which you feel you can logically support or prove.

▓ **Define** any terms which may be unclear.

▓ **Support** your point with evidence which is interesting and reliable.

▓ **Explain** why your audience should accept your evidence.

▓ **Consider** any objections your audience could have to your explanation.

▓ **Admit** that some arguments against your point may be true.

▓ **Point out** the weaknesses in those arguments you do not accept.

▓ **Restate** your central claim or point.

▓ **Urge** your audience to accept your viewpoint.

Helpful HINT
You will probably not use every one of these stages each time you set out to prove a point. Each situation is different and requires some creative thinking and common sense as well as logic and reason.

The thorough discussion of logical thinking will help young learners think and write persuasively. The many helpful hints provide young learners with special insights into thinking, writing, speaking, listening, reading, etc.

Thinking Creatively 334

What if . . . ?
334

The best creative thinkers see things differently than the people around them. They see challenges rather than problems. They set aside all the rules, all the scorecards, all of what is usually expected, and begin to imagine "What would happen if . . . ?" If you sometimes find it hard to imagine, to go beyond the correct or obvious answer, maybe the suggestions below will help.

▓ **What if** a certain person, place, thing, or idea did not exist today? What if it suddenly appeared 100 years before its time? (What if the airplane had not yet been invented? What if it had been invented before the Civil War?)

▓ **What if** people did things differently than they do? (What if everyone spoke whenever they felt like it and said whatever they wanted? What if no one collected our garbage?)

▓ **What if** the world were different in some important way? (What if the sun were to shine only two hours a day? 20 hours a day? What if it rained only twice a year? every day?)

▓ **What if** two people, things, or ideas which are usually separate were brought together? (Parents and rock musicians? Tomatoes and ice cream?)

▓ **What if** you were to change just one important thing about an object or machine? (Change the ink in every pen to green? Cut the size of the gas tanks on all cars to one-fourth their current size?)

"Most people see things as they are and ask, "Why?" I see things that never were and ask "Why not?"
—**Robert F. Kennedy**

▓ **What if** a certain object could talk? (Your shoe? Your house? A newborn baby?)

▓ **What if** a certain object were made of another material? (Metal car tires? Grass clothes? Cardboard furniture?)

▓ **What if** a certain person, place, object, or idea were the "opposite" of what he, she, or it is now? (What is George Bush became Georgia Bush? Homes became schools? Cars became helicopters? Forward became backward?)

▓ **What if** a certain object were suddenly very scarce or plentiful? (What if there were suddenly very little paper? Plenty of money?)

▓ **What if** a certain object were a totally different size? (2-foot pens? 9-foot baskets?)

▓ **What if** . . .

Students who find it hard to imagine or see beyond obvious answers will be enlightened by this and other pages in the chapter on creative thinking.

Write Source 2000 encourages students to personalize and actively pursue learning. The chapter on interviewing will help students learn from people in their community.

405

Interviewing

One of the most valuable sources of information available to people today is other people. And the best way to get good, current information from other people is to sit down and talk to them and listen to what they have to say. This is what newspaper, magazine, and television people do everyday. You, too, should consider interviewing others whenever you are asked to find information or research a topic. The tips which follow should help make your interview more comfortable and successful.

405   **Tips for Better Interviewing**

Before the Interview . . .

- Select a person to interview who has special knowledge or personal experiences to share.
- Write out all the questions you would like to ask. (Phrase your questions so that your subject cannot answer with just a "yes" or "no.")
- Make an appointment for a time and place which is convenient for the person you are going to interview.
- Let your subject know beforehand what kind of project you are working on and what topics you hope to cover. (You might even tell him or her some of the questions so he or she has time to think about them.)
- Study your topic as much as possible before the interview so that you are not likely to be overwhelmed with new information.
- Practice with your tape recorder beforehand so that you know how to change batteries, tapes, and sides of the tape. Label your tapes

---

Taking Tests   418-419

Taking Tests

The key to doing well in school is simple—be involved and be prepared. This is never more true than when you are about to be tested on what you have learned. The guidelines which follow should help as you begin your preparation.

Test-Taking Skills

Organizing and Preparing Test Material ▬▬▬▬▬ **418**

Ask questions . . .

- What will be on the test? Ask the teacher to be as specific as possible.
- How will the material be tested? (multiple choice? essay?)

Organize your notes . . .

- Review your class notes carefully.
- Get any notes or materials you may have missed from the teacher or another student.

Think about the test . . .

- Gather old quizzes and exams.
- Prepare an outline of everything to be covered on the test.
- Set aside a list of any questions you need to ask the teacher or another student.

Reviewing and Remembering Test Material ▬▬▬▬▬ **419**

Begin studying early . . .

- Set up a specific time to study for an exam and stick to it.
- Begin reviewing early. Don't wait until the night before a test.
- Skim the material in your textbooks and make a list of special terms and ideas to study; copy over notes of the most important areas.

All students need help when it comes to studying. The chapter on test taking is one of many that helps students manage and make the most of their course work.

Prefixes   374

Prefixes

374

Prefixes are those "word parts" which come *before* the root word (pre=before). Prefixes often change the meaning of a word from positive to negative, or negative to positive. As a skilled reader, you will want to know the meaning of the most common prefixes and then watch for them when you read.

a, an [*not, without*] amoral (without a sense of moral responsibility), atypical, atom (not cutable), apathy (without feeling)

ab, abs, a [*from, away*] abnormal, avert (turn away), abduct

acro [*high*] acropolis (high city), acrobat, acronym, acrophobia (fear of height)

ad, ac, af, ag, al, an, ap, ar, as, at [*to, towards*] admire (look at with wonder), attract, admit, advance, allege, announce, assert, aggressive, accept

ambi, amb [*both, around*] ambidextrous (skilled with both hands), ambiguous, amble

amphi [*both*] amphibious (living on both land and water), amphitheater

ana [*on, up, backward*] analysis (loosening up or taking apart for study), anatomy

ante [*before*] antedate, anteroom, antebellum, antecedent (happening before)

anti, ant [*against*] anticommunist, antidote, anticlimax, antacid

apo [*from, off*] apostasy (standing from, abandoning a professed belief), apology, apothecary, apostle

be [*on, away*] bedeck, belabor, bequest, bestow, beloved

bene, bon [*well*] benefit, bonus, benefactor, benevolent, benediction, bonanza

bi, bis, bin [*both, double, twice*] bicycle, biweekly, binoculars, bilateral, biscuit

by [*side, close, near*] bypass, bystander, by-product, bylaw, byline

cata [*down, against*] catalogue, catapult, catastrophe, cataclysm

cerebro [*brain*] cerebral, cerebrum, cerebellum

circum, circ [*around*] circumference, circumnavigate, circumspect

co, con, col, cor, com [*together, with*] compose, copilot, conspire, collect, concord

contra, counter [*against*] controversy, contradict, counterpart

de [*from, down*] demote, depress, degrade, deject, deprive

deca [*ten*] decade, decathlon, decapod (ten feet)

di [*two, twice*] divide, dilemma, dilute

dia [*through, between*] diameter, diagonal, diagram, dialogue (speech between people)

dis, dif [*apart, away, reverse*] dismiss, distort, distinguish, diffuse

dys [*badly, ill*] dyspepsia (digesting badly, indigestion), dystrophy, dysentery

em, en [*in, into*] embrace, enslave

eu, ev [*well*] eulogize (speak well of, praise), eupepsia, euphony, eugenics

epi [*upon*] epidermis (upon the skin, outer layer of skin), epitaph, epithet

ex, e, ec, ef [*out*] expel (drive out), ex-mayor, exit, exorcism, eccentric (out of the center position), eject, emit

extra, extro [*beyond, outside*] extraordinary (beyond the ordinary), extracurricular, extrovert

fore [*before in time*] forecast, foretell (to tell beforehand), foreshadow, foregone, forefather

hemi, demi, semi [*half*] hemisphere, hemicycle, semicircle (half of a circle), demitasse

hex [*six*] hexameter, hexagon

homo [*man*] Homo sapiens, homicide (killing man)

hyper [*over, above*] hypersensitive (overly sensitive), hypertensive, hyperactive

hypo [*under*] hypodermic (under the skin), hypothesis

idio [*private, personal*] idiom, idiosyncrasy, idiomatic

il, ir, in, im [*not*] incorrect, illegal, immoral, irregular

in, il, im [*into*] inject, inside, illuminate, impose, illustrate, implant, imprison

infra [*beneath*] infrared

inter [*between*] intercollegiate, interfere, intervene, interrupt (break between)

intra [*within*] intramural, intravenous (within the veins)

intro [*into, inward*] introduce, introvert (turn inward)

The dictionary of prefixes, suffixes, and roots provides your students with a handy resource for vocabulary building.

A special color-coded section called "The Yellow Pages" answers any questions students may have about mechanics, grammar, and usage. Graphic "see references" point students to additional information.

Understanding Sentences 695-697

The Yellow Pages Guide to
Understanding
Sentences

There is little doubt that the sentence is the cornerstone of all writing. Whether we like it or not, we are expected to use *sentences*—not sentence fragments, run-ons, or spliced sentences—but complete, colorful, concise, correct sentences in a variety of shapes and sizes. As you practice and experiment with your sentences, it might be helpful for you to know how different kinds of sentences are put together and what the various sentence "elements" are. The information in this section should help.

Sentence
695

A **sentence** is made up of one or more words which express a complete thought. (*Note:* A sentence begins with a capital letter; it ends with a period, question mark, or exclamation point.)

This book should help you write. It explains many things.

How do you plan to use it? I hope you find it helpful!

 For more information on sentences, turn to "Composing Sentences," 090-114, in your handbook.

WORDS IN A SENTENCE

Subject & Predicate 696
◆ A sentence must have a subject and predicate in order to express a complete thought. Either the subject or the predicate (or both) may *not* be stated, but both must be clearly understood.

[*You*] **Join our union!** [*You* is the understood subject.]

Who needs independence? People. [*do*] [*Do* is the understood predicate.]

What can you lose by joining? [*We can lose*] **Freedom.** [*We* is the understood subject, and *can lose* is the understood predicate.]

Subject 697
◆ A subject is the part of a sentence which is doing something or about which something is said.

In 1940 *Russia* took away the independence and identities of the Baltic states. Now *they* are finally regaining their freedom.

459-465   Marking Punctuation

Period
459

A **period** is used to end a sentence which makes a statement or a request, or which gives a command which is not used as an exclamation.

Try these car facts on for size. [Command]

Cars of the future will come with electronic navigation systems. [Statement]

Video rearview mirrors will relay the "rear view" on an in-dash video screen. [Statement]

Relax. [Request]

In-car radar systems (they can scan up to 400 feet) will help you avoid head-on collisions. [Statement]

Note: It is not necessary to place a period after a statement which has parentheses around it and is part of another sentence.

460 .... After an Initial
◆ A period should be placed after an initial.

M. E. Kerr [writer]

Steven P. Jobs [founder of Apple computers]

461 .... As a Decimal
◆ Use a period as a decimal point and to separate dollars and cents.

Experts are 69.9 percent sure (okay 70 percent) that a pill now under development will prevent cavities and cost about $9.50 each.

At the End of a Sentence 462
◆ When an abbreviation is the last word in a sentence, only one period should be used at the end of the sentence.

By the year 2030, a 65-year-old individual may be as fit as a 45-year-old person today because of advances in nutrition, exercise, preventative medicine, etc.

After Abbreviations 463
◆ A period is placed after each part of an abbreviation—unless the abbreviation is an acronym. An acronym is a word formed from the first (or first few) letters of words in a set phrase. (See 556.)

Abbreviations .... Mr., Mrs., Ms., Dr., A.D., B.C.
Acronyms .... BASIC, DOS, laser, modem

Ellipsis
464

An ellipsis (three periods) may be used to indicate a pause in dialogue or to show omitted words or sentences. (When typing, leave one space before, after, and between each period.)

To Show a Pause 465
◆ An ellipsis is used to indicate a pause in dialogue.

"Why did I get home late, Dad? Well, Jill and I . . . ah . . . yeah, were in another galaxy. Well, I . . . ah . . . mean we were watching *2001: A Space Odyssey* on Jill's new 3-D TV."

563-567   Spelling

Spelling
563

564 .... i before e
◆ Write *i* before *e* except after *c*, or when sounded like *a* as in *neighbor* and *weigh*.

Exceptions: Eight of the exceptions are in this sentence:

Neither sheik dared leisurely seize either weird species of financiers.

Note: Other exceptions to the *i* before *e* rule are *their, height, counterfeit, foreign,* and *heir*.

565 .... Silent e
◆ If a word ends with a silent *e*, drop the *e* before adding a suffix which begins with a vowel.

state — stating — statement
like — liking — likeness
use — using — useful
nine — ninety — nineteen

(Notice that you do *not* drop the *e* when the suffix begins with a consonant. Exceptions include *truly, argument,* and *ninth*.)

Words Ending in Y 566
◆ When *y* is the last letter in a word and the *y* comes just after a consonant, change the *y* to *i* before adding any suffix except those beginning with *i*.

fry — fries, hurry — hurried, lady — ladies, ply — pliable, happy — happiness, beauty — beautiful

◆ When forming the plural of a word which ends with a *y* that comes just after a vowel, add *s*.

toy — toys, play — plays, monkey — monkeys

Consonant Ending 567
◆ When a one-syllable word (bat) ends in a consonant (bat) preceded by one vowel (bat), double the final consonant before adding a suffix which begins with a vowel (batting).

◆ When a multi-syllable word (control) ends in a consonant (l) preceded by one vowel (o), the accent is on the last syllable (control), and the suffix begins with a vowel (ing)—the same rule holds true: double the final consonant (controlling).

sum — summary
god — goddess
prefer — preferred
begin — beginning

SCHOOL DAZE

*Gee Ms. Roberts, if I have to cut any more **misspelled** words, the only thing left will be my name!*

 The examples given throughout "The Yellow Pages" are entertaining, colorful, and informative. In the chapter on punctuation, each example presents an interesting and thought-provoking look at the future.

The "School Daze" comic strips which appear throughout this section not only illustrate important concepts, but also provide an entertaining look at school life.

Tables and Lists 797

Tables and Lists

The tables, charts, and lists which follow should be both interesting to use and helpful to have at your fingertips. Everything from "Animal Facts" to the "Periodic Table of the Elements" is worth knowing and may be expected of you in some class at some time. We hope the variety of information is both useful and fun.

Animal Facts 797

Animal	Male	Female	Young	Group	Gestation	Longevity
Bear	He-bear	She-bear	Cub	Sleuth	180-240	18-20 (34)
Cat	Tom	Queen	Kitten	Clutter/Clowder	52-65	10-17 (30)
Cattle	Bull	Cow	Calf	Drove/Herd	280	9-12 (25)
Chicken	Rooster	Hen	Chick	Brood/Flock	21	7-8 (14)
Deer	Buck	Doe	Fawn	Herd	180-250	10-15 (26)
Dog	Dog	Bitch	Pup	Pack/Kennel	55-70	10-12 (24)
Donkey	Jack	Jenny	Foal	Herd/Pace	340-385	18-20 (63)*
Duck	Drake	Duck	Duckling	Brace/Herd	21-35	10 (15)
Elephant	Bull	Cow	Calf	Herd	515-760	30-60 (98)
Fox	Dog	Vixen	Cub/Kit	Skulk	51-60	8-10 (14)
Goat	Billy	Nanny	Kid	Tribe/Herd	135-163	12 (17)
Goose	Gander	Goose	Gosling	Flock/Gaggle	30	25-30
Horse	Stallion	Mare	Filly/Colt	Herd	304-419	20-30 (50+)
Lion	Lion	Lioness	Cub	Pride	105-111	10 (29)
Monkey	Male	Female	Boy/Girl	Band/Troop	149-179	12-15 (29)
Rabbit	Buck	Doe	Bunny	Nest/Warren	27-36	6-8 (15)
Sheep	Ram	Ewe	Lamb	Flock/Drove	121-180	10-15 (16)
Swan	Cob	Pen	Cygnet	Bevy/Flock	30	45-50
Swine	Boar	Sow	Piglet	Litter/Herd	101-130	10 (15)
Tiger	Tiger	Tigress	Cub		105	19
Whale	Bull	Cow	Calf	Gam/Pod/Herd	276-365	37
Wolf	Dog	Bitch	Pup	Pack	63	10-12 (16)

* ( ) Record for oldest animal of this type

◀ **"The Student Almanac"** allows *Write Source 2000* to work across the curriculum with informative tables and charts like **"Animal Facts."**

All About Maps 826-828

All About Maps

As you know, the world has changed dramatically in the past several years. As global citizens it is up to each of us to stay on top of those changes. Just as we once tried to understand something about each of the 50 states, we must now work to understand each of the 170 countries in the world. The section which follows will give you the map skills you need to begin your work.

Kinds of Maps 826

Maps have many uses, and there are as many different kinds of maps as there are uses. Your handbook uses one kind of map, the *political map*. Political maps show how the earth is divided into countries and states. Often they also show the capitals and major cities. The different sizes and styles of the print (or type) used for names on the maps are also important. These are clues to help make the map information clear. Usually, the most important names are typed in the largest print. Different kinds of type are used for countries, cities, rivers, lakes, and other places.

Using the Maps 827

Mapmakers use special marks and symbols to show where things are or to give other useful information. Among other things, these marks and symbols show direction (north, south, east, and west).

On most maps, north is at the top. But you should always check the *compass rose* or *directional finder* to make sure you know where north is. If there is no symbol, you can assume that north is at the top.

The Legend 828

Other important marks and symbols are explained in a box printed on each map. This box is called the *legend* or *key*. It is included to make it easier for you to understand and use the map. Here is the map legend for North America. It includes a map scale and symbols for capitals and boundary lines.

```
          NORTH AMERICA
  0            1000 Km
  0                      1000 Mi.
  National Capitals          ○
  Provincial and Territorial Capitals   ●
  International Boundaries    ——
  © Write Source Publishing House
```

▲ **Up-to-date, full-color maps are included in this section along with helpful guidelines for using the maps.**

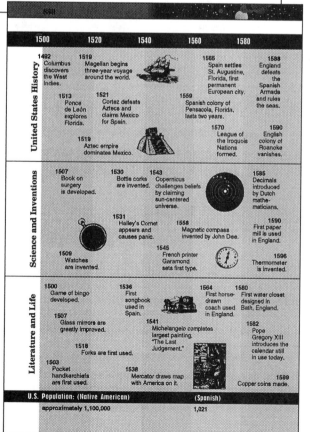

	1500	1520	1540	1560	1580

United States History

1492 Columbus discovers the West Indies.

1513 Ponce de León explores Florida.

1519 Magellan begins three-year voyage around the world.

1521 Cortez defeats Aztecs and claims Mexico for Spain.

1519 Aztec empire dominates Mexico.

1565 Spain settles St. Augustine, Florida, first permanent European city.

1559 Spanish colony of Pensacola, Florida, lasts two years.

1570 League of the Iroquois Nations formed.

1588 England defeats the Spanish Armada and rules the seas.

1590 English colony of Roanoke vanishes.

Science and Inventions

1507 Book on surgery is developed.

1509 Watches are invented.

1530 Bottle corks are invented.

1531 Halley's Comet appears and causes panic.

1543 Copernicus challenges beliefs by claiming sun-centered universe.

1558 Magnetic compass invented by John Dee.

1545 French printer Garamond sets first type.

1585 Decimals introduced by Dutch mathematicians.

1590 First paper mill is used in England.

1596 Thermometer is invented.

Literature and Life

1500 Game of bingo developed.

1507 Glass mirrors are greatly improved.

1503 Pocket handkerchiefs are first used.

1518 Forks are first used.

1536 First songbook used in Spain.

1541 Michelangelo completes largest painting, "The Last Judgement."

1538 Mercator draws map with America on it.

1564 First horse-drawn coach used in England.

1580 First water closet designed in Bath, England.

1582 Pope Gregory XIII introduces the calendar still in use today.

1599 Copper coins made.

U.S. Population: (Native American) approximately 1,100,000   **(Spanish)** 1,021

◀ The **"Historical Time Line"** helps students better understand important and interesting events from the past. The events in the time line are organized into three categories: United States History, Science and Inventions, and Literature and Life.

A Closer Look

The following pages contain

a section by section overview of

WS 2000 with specific suggestions

and helpful hints for using

the handbook in your classroom.

Write Source 2000

Section by Section Teacher's Notes

Writing to Learn

Rationale: We know how many students approach writing. They begin each writing project with one idea in mind—completing it. They aim straight for the finish line and bypass all of the interesting twists and turns each project has to offer. All of their energy goes into producing something to turn in, something as free of careless errors as they can make it, and, unfortunately, something that falls far short of what they are capable of producing.

Our purpose in "Writing to Learn" is to direct your students' enthusiasm and energy in the right direction, so they can produce writing that they feel good about and you and your students can enjoy reading. (We were teachers ourselves, so we know it's no picnic reading a set of "who can get to the finish line first" pieces of writing.)

Chapter Summaries

Writing to Learn (004-010)

Students need to know that writing is much more than just another assignment. They need to see writing not only as an effective learning tool, but also as an important part of a satisfying life—right up there with exercise and a well-balanced diet. That's our purpose in this short chapter—to help students appreciate what writing has to offer them.

We identify six different types of learning that can be enhanced by putting pen to paper. By writing, students can better learn about themselves, their immediate world, their acquaintances, LIFE (as in the big picture), their course work, and their initial ideas for writing assignments.

Helpful HINT
If your students are reluctant writers, try this one on them: Tell them that if they write regularly in and out of school, they will get better grades. They won't necessarily turn into straight A students, but they can't help but improve their grades if they follow our advice for personal and school-related writing in this chapter as well as throughout the handbook.

Getting Started: To help students experience writing as a personal learning tool, we open with "An Invitation to Writing." Have students "lift off" into writing with this activity before you read and discuss the rest of the chapter.

Enrichment: If you want your students to begin writing in a personal journal after reading and discussing "Writing to Learn," see 130 in the handbook for guidelines.

The Writing Process (011-027)

No one—not even the most accomplished writer—gets his writing right the first time. Writing must go through a process or series of steps before it's ready to share with readers. Your challenge—and the challenge of all teachers who have their students write—is to make sure that your students appreciate this fact as well. "The Writing Process" is designed to help you meet this challenge.

"Writing in Action" (011), the introduction to "The Writing Process," describes for your students how professional writers develop a piece of writing. What follows is an explanation of the steps in the writing process and how your students can make use of these steps when they develop their own writing.

Helpful HINT
Make sure that your students understand that a writer does not progress in a linear fashion through the steps in the writing process. There is a lot of forward and backward motion. As writing researcher Sandra Perl states, "People go back to the words on the page in order to move forward."

Getting Started: Before you read and discuss any part of "The Writing Process," have your students describe their personal "process" of writing—that is, the way in which they have generally completed writing assignments in the past. Compare this process to the one described in this chapter. Later in the quarter, have students describe how their personal process of writing has changed after working with *Write Source 2000* for a few of their writing projects.

Special Points of Interest:

012 "The Steps in the Process" (These steps serve as the focus for all of the forms of writing discussed in *Write Source 2000.*)

017 "Focusing Your Efforts" (Students must understand that they don't have to say everything in their writing.)

021 "Connecting: Revising Your Writing" (What student doesn't need help and advice with revising?)

027 "Correcting and Proofreading Checklist" (Students should always refer to this checklist when they are putting the finishing touches on their writing.)

Enrichment: Have students in pairs list at least four or five important things they remember to do when they write.

■ Here are some things we feel are important for you and your students to remember about writing. (You might want to refer to our ideas during the discussion of your students' lists.)

❑ Writing should be approached as a process of discovery, not as an end product.

❑ Writers should write about something that interests them.

❑ Writers should be knowledgeable about the subject of their writing.

❑ Writers should share their work throughout the writing process.

❑ Writers should write for an intended audience, even if that means their fellow writers.

❑ Writers should write in an honest and sincere voice.

Note: Post a list of "Keys to Good Writing" in your classroom where all of your students can see it. And remind students to refer to this list whenever they are developing a piece of writing. (Make changes in the list as the year progresses.)

Group Advising (028-029)

Writers need to talk about their writing with fellow writers. That's why writing groups are so important. They promote a writing community in your classroom, and they promote the give and take of writing ideas which will help your students grow as writers. "Group Advising" provides you and your students with guidelines for conducting productive sharing sessions.

> *"Sharing allows writers to hear what their ideas sound like and to solicit feedback as they continue to think about a topic, draft, or revise."*
> —Karen Spear

Getting Started: Have students write freely for 10 minutes about anything they wish. (Refer them to 039-041 for writing ideas.) Then have them share their free writing with a classmate using the "Writing Group Guidelines" (028). Instruct listeners to make at least one positive comment and ask at least two questions which would help the writers further develop their writing.

Where do you go from here? Have students work their initial free writings into finished pieces (with the help of the handbook and their classmates in group advising sessions). Or have them move on to another type of writing for additional group practice.

 "Stage" at least one group advising session before your students read and react to each other's writing.

Special Points of Interest:

029 "Commenting on Writing" (Students will find this checklist helpful when they review each other's writing.)

432 "Group Skills" (This chapter provides insights into effective group skills.)

Enrichment: Give your students practice with evaluating writing using the peer editing minilesson on page 57 in this booklet.

Starting Points (030-041)

"Starting Points" summarizes the steps in the writing process and follows with a number of stimulating prewriting ideas which will help your students search for and shape subjects for almost any type of writing. According to some researchers, at least one third of a student's time during a writing project should be devoted to prewriting and inventing.

 Free writing, listing, and clustering are three effective ways to explore and discover through writing. Give your students plenty of practice using these prewriting techniques.

Getting Started: Use the minilesson "Alphabet Cluster" (page 103 in this booklet) to give your students clustering practice. Or, use the minilesson "Twenty-Five Steps" (page 102) to get your students right into free writing.

Enrichment: Early in the year, have your students generate a "SourceBank" of personal writing ideas by developing a "Personal Almanac" or a "Life Map" (034). Provide students with large sheets of paper for their life maps.

The Basic Elements of Writing

Rationale: Student writers should make decisions about their work based on the meaning that is evolving in units or large chunks of writing. That is why "The Basic Elements of Writing" opens with discussions of whole compositions—essays and paragraphs—and follows with discussions of sentences.

Developing Essays (043-074)

Two general types of essays—the personal essay and the school essay—are discussed in detail in this section. The discussion of the personal essay presents an open-ended look at essay writing—the essay as a catch-all personal form of writing. The discussion of the school essay presents a traditional look at essay writing—complete with outlines and thesis statements. This section concludes with guidelines for writing two-part essays (as in comparison and contrast essays) and guidelines for writing essays about people, places, objects, events, and so on.

Getting Started: Before you discuss the guidelines for writing personal essays, have students retrace their actions during part of a typical school day. Tell them that in doing this they are creating a number of possible ideas for a special type of writing. (See 046 for a model. Also take note of the Helpful Hint on that page. You might want to have your students work on this activity instead.)

Where do you go from here? Have your students develop one of their ideas into a personal essay after reviewing with them the guidelines in *Write Source 2000*. Or have them save these ideas in their writing folders for use in the future.

Special Points of Interest:

044 "Writing the Personal Essay" (This form of writing may be new to your students; the school essay will not be.)
058 "Personalizing the School Essay" (Students can add some spark to their school essays with the ideas presented on this page.)
064-074 (These guidelines will help students develop a variety of essay types. Make sure you review them sometime during the first quarter.)

Enrichment: There's nothing like a good gripe session to cleanse the spleen. Have your students sound off with their own pet peeves. (See 050.)

Building Paragraphs (075-089)

Everything you and your students need to know about paragraphs (and then some) is included in this section.

If your students' writing generally lacks specific details and examples, make sure they read and react to "The Details in a Paragraph" (082-085). It might provide the right cure for this common writing ailment.

Getting Started: Before or during an introductory discussion, have your students think metaphorically about paragraphs and develop "A paragraph is like . . ." statements. For example, a paragraph is like a hamburger—the more you add between the buns, the better it tastes. Or, a paragraph is the middle child of prose, not necessarily as mature as an essay or whole composition but more developed than an individual sentence. These statements should be shared and made part of a class discussion.

Special Points of Interest:

084 "Methods of Arranging Details" (Students will find this list a handy resource for all of their expository writing.)
087 "Reviewing Paragraphs in Essays, Reports, and Longer Pieces of Writing" (With the guidelines on this page, students can make sure that each of their paragraphs works in longer pieces of writing.)
089 "Transition or Linking Words" (Students will find this chart another handy writing resource.)

Enrichment: Give your students the following challenge: Write a paragraph which includes the following levels of detail: (See 085 in the handbook.)

  (1) Controlling (Topic) sentence
    (2) Clarifying sentence
      (3) Completing sentence
      (3) Completing sentence (Optional)
    (2) Clarifying sentence
      (3) Completing sentence
      (3) Completing sentence (Optional)
  (1) Controlling (Closing) sentence

Note: This is only a suggested pattern for this paragraph. Adjust it to meet the needs of your students.

Composing, Combining, and Styling Sentences (090-114)

When a student writer is ready to edit his work, one of the first things he should do is check his writing sentence by sentence. He should make sure that each sentence expresses a complete thought, that it reads smoothly, and that it is worded in the best possible way. These three chapters on sentences will provide your students with all they need to know when they are reviewing and fine-tuning the sentences in their writing.

Getting Started: Put students into groups of three. Instruct two students to talk about a movie they have both seen, a book they have both read, a game they have both participated in, etc. The third member of the group must listen carefully and record the conversation as it unfolds. (A tape recorder will be a big help for the transcriber.)

Where do you go from here? The transcriptions can be utilized in any number of ways as you read and react to these chapters on sentences. You might, for example, ask each group to volunteer examples of specific sentence errors from their transcriptions when you discuss "Composing Sentences."

Special Points of Interest:

094 "Write 'Agreeable' Sentences" (Remind your students to turn to these pages on common agreement errors whenever they edit their writing.)

102 "Combining Sentences" (This chapter will help students write smoother, more detailed sentences.)

109 "Developing a Sense of Style" (This segment will help students really practice the art of writing.)

Enrichment: Have students keep a file of sentences with style, sentences that are particularly well put in the work of their classmates and from the books and magazines that they read. Encourage students to use these types of sentences in their own writing.

A Special Challenge:

> *"As a general rule, run your pen through every other word you have written; you have no idea what vigor it will give to your writing style."*
> **—Sydney Smith**

Have your students follow Sydney Smith's advice for a recent piece of writing. (They don't, however, have to literally cut every other word.) Then see what they can make of their writing after the cutting.

The Art of Writing

Rationale: Professional writers write to discover something new and worthwhile to share with their readers. This has to be the foremost purpose in the mind of anyone who writes, including your students. As writer Donald Murray says, "If the writer does not feel that through writing he will discover something which is uniquely his, he may soon concentrate on craft rather than content." Does this mean that craft is unimportant? Absolutely not. If a writer has something worthwhile to say, he will naturally want to share his ideas as effectively as he can.

The guidelines and advice throughout *Write Source 2000* will help your students find something worthwhile to say in their writing. The advice and guidelines in "The Art of Writing" will help them "speak their piece" in an effective and entertaining way.

> *"I believe in impulse and naturalness, but followed by discipline in the cutting."*
> **—Anaïs Nin**

Chapter Summaries
Writing Naturally (116-117)

Students become writers once they acquire a real feel for writing and develop their natural writing voice. They can best do this by generating a lot of writing—especially the type that is free from the gravitational pull of a teacher's red pen. This is a good reason to get your students writing regularly in a personal journal. Read on in the chapter for more helpful hints.

Getting Started: Have students select a writing prompt (039) to write about freely for five to ten minutes. Have pairs of students exchange papers and make note of sections of their partner's paper that sound especially honest, sincere, and natural.

Enrichment: On slips of paper, write *best friend, teacher, parent, uncle, grandmother,* etc. and have students pick one of the slips. Then instruct them to write a friendly letter to this person. (The subject of the letter can be what the writer did over the past weekend.) You and your students should find that the intended audience affects a writer's natural writing voice. For example, the voice a student uses when writing to a best friend will be different than the voice used when writing to a grandparent.

Improving Your Writing (118-123)

*"Those marvelous English mono-syllables. . . .
Who could improve on splash, smash, ooze,
shriek, slush, glide, squeak, coo? Who could
think of anything more sloppy than slop? And
what could be more peremptory than stop?"*
—Arville Schaleben

Splash, smash, ooze, shriek, slush—all wonderful words, the type of colorful and power-packed words you want your students to use in their writing. The guidelines in "Improving Your Writing" will help your students review their writing for word choice so they include, among other things, many of the "marvelous English mono-syllables."

Getting Started: Have students pantomime strong, colorful words. (See "Pantomime Vocabulary Builder," page 88 in this booklet, for guidelines.) You will need a set of thesauruses for this activity.

Enrichment: Have students complete the minilesson "Why We Hiccup" (page 104 in this booklet). Remind students that the word choice in each of their explanations should reflect the age and experience of their writing personas.

A Special Challenge: Have your students submit boring paragraphs, paragraphs with no life in them, paragraphs that hang limp like wet wash. Redistribute the paragraphs so students get new ones. Then have them rewrite these duds using "How do you really know what to change?" (123) as their guide.

Writing Techniques and Writing Terms (124-128)

Every possible writing technique and term your students will need to know is listed in these two chapters.

Getting Started: How can you best use this information? Pick and choose those techniques and terms you want your students to know and use. Make a master list for yourself. Then make these words the focus of writing lessons throughout the school year.

Enrichment: Make pairs of students responsible for presenting minilessons on various techniques and terms. For example, you might have one group provide an explanation and examples of parallelism, another group present information on cliches, and still another group present information on sarcasm.

Personal Writing

Rationale: "Personal Writing" is the first in a series of three sections which catalog a variety of writing forms.

You and your students can put this information to use in any number of ways. You might use this information to plan a basic writing program by selecting those writing forms you want your students to work with throughout the year. If you conduct a writing workshop, you can rest assured that the information in these sections will provide your students all the help they need with most of their writing projects. And if you're simply looking for guidelines for a certain form of writing, you'll probably find them in one of these three sections.

The types of writing in the first two sections progress from very personal types to writing that is gradually more remote, more public in form. The final section describes many creative forms of writing. A lot of our thinking about what forms to include in these sections and in what sequence can be attributed to James Moffett's approach to writing in *Active Voices* (Heinemann-Boynton/Cook, 1981).

Included in "Personal Writing" are guidelines for keeping a personal journal as well as guidelines for writing phase autobiographies and autobiographical incidents (writing about experiences). Also included are samples of additional forms of personal writing your students might want to work with.

*"Writing is not apart from living.
Writing is a kind of double living."*
—Catherine Brinker Bower

Chapter Summaries
Journal Writing (130-132)

We can't think of a more painless and productive way for students to practice writing than doing so in a personal journal. Read and react to 006-010 as well as 130-131 with your students before they begin their journal writing. And make sure that you provide them with the proper send-off for their first journal entry (see 004-005).

Getting Started: Have pairs of students develop a dialogue journal (132) for at least a week. This is an effective beginning-of-the-year activity. Encourage classmates to continue their "conversations" on their own after the week is up.

Enrichment: Have students keep track of their journal writing progress on a chart like the one below.

Date	Topic	Writing Time	Number of Words	Comment

Possible Comments
A. Continue writing on this topic.
B. Continue writing on this topic but from a different angle.
C. Write on a related topic.
D. Write on a topic which unexpectedly developed.
E. Go on to another topic.

Writing Phase Autobiographies (133-143)

Most of today's students spend little time reflecting about their past. And small wonder. They are busy enough living life in the present. You can help your students forget about the present for awhile and think about earlier times in their lives by having them write phase autobiographies.

 If your students are not sure what you mean by a "phase" in their lives, have them read and react to the model phase autobiographies in the handbook (141-142).

Getting Started: The listing activity (135) provides an easy and effective way for students to recall past experiences. Of course, this activity only becomes important if your students have difficulty thinking of a phase to write about.
Note: You might have pairs of students alternate "I remember" statements and work from each other's ideas.

Enrichment: Have your students think of their phase autobiographies as one chapter in their personal stories. Instruct them to think of other important chapters in their lives and create a table of contents for their complete autobiographies.

 See the "Minilessons" section (pages 93-110) for additional activities.

Writing About Experiences (144-149)

It's natural and easy for students to talk about their experiences. And it's not hard for them to write about these experiences either. This is one type of writing almost all of my students enjoyed writing and sharing with their classmates. You'll find writing about experiences to be a perfect activity for early in the year.
Note: This type of writing is known by a number of names, including the autobiographical incident paper and the personal narrative.

Getting Started: Prior to assigning a personal experience paper, have students write a series of journal entries which focus on their experiences. (See 039 in the handbook for writing prompts.) They then have a valuable "SourceBank" of writing ideas to choose from.

Enrichment: Have students praise or bury a memorable object in a brief speech. Let your students' imaginations run wild here. They could prepare a eulogy, a campaign speech, an ode, an article for the obituary column, and so on. (See 070 and 389 in the handbook for guidelines.)

Subject Writing

Rationale: Young writers enjoy writing about their own lives and benefit greatly from the experience. But they also need plenty of practice writing about subjects other than themselves. That's why we've developed this extensive section called "Subject Writing." This section provides information on any number of forms of writing, all of which focus on subjects other than the writer. Included are a variety of guidelines from writing about other people in phase biographies to writing to people in friendly letters, from writing about places of interest in observation reports to writing about books in book reviews.

"Good writing is filled with specific, accurate, honest information. The reader is persuaded through authoritative information that the writer knows the subject."
—Donald Murray

Writing Phase Biographies (151-158)

A phase biography will take your students beyond their own memories into the lives of relatives, friends, or figures from the past. It offers them a chance to continue the detailing and shaping they learned while writing phase autobiographies. In addition, it offers them a chance to practice interviewing, note taking, and informal researching. Defining a "phase" gives students a chance to practice shaping nonfiction writing to illustrate and support a main idea or focus.

Getting Started: Have your students search for possible writing subjects by free-writing about interesting relatives, ancestors, or acquaintances. Also, have them read and react to "Francis Ann Slocum" (157) as well as to the introductory material (151-154) before they begin developing their phase biographies.

Helpful HINT Students will need to learn about and practice interviewing for this type of writing. (See 405-407 for guidelines.) Have your students conduct mock interviews in your class. Also, consider having a news reporter or some other experienced interviewer share his or her insights on interviewing with your class.

Enrichment: Once your students complete their phase biographies, consider the following activity: Change the point of view of your phase biography so it becomes a phase autobiography—that is, so the subject tells his or her own story. Does this mean that your students should completely rewrite their papers? No, have them do something a little different. Perhaps they could develop a "phase auto-poem" by adjusting the guidelines for a bio-poem (158) so it reads as if personally written by the subject of the poem.

Character Sketch (159-165)

A *phase biography* presents only a significant slice of a person's life. Generally, a *character sketch* presents a subject as he or she is now, in toto. (Whatever needs to be explained, described, and shared in a sketch, is . . . so the readers get a good feel for the subject.)

The phase biographer asks himself, "How can I best share with my readers an important time in my subject's life?" While the writer of a character sketch asks himself, "How can I effectively share the 'big picture' of who this person is?"

The phase biographer starts with a certain framework already in place—a period of time in the subject's life. The writer of a character sketch has no such framework. He must pick and choose from the facts and details he has gathered and establish his own parameters.

Getting Started: The minilesson "Eyes Like Meteors" (see page 105 in this booklet) provides an effective starting point for this project.

Helpful HINT Remind your students to be careful when they choose details to include in their sketches. They shouldn't say anything that unnecessarily hurts their subjects' feelings. Whenever possible, students should get a potential subject's permission before starting out.

Enrichment: Explain the guidelines for this activity a day ahead of time, so they can prepare pantomimes to go along with their character sketches.

Ask students to select a passage, an incident, a characteristic action, etc. from their sketches to pantomime. When called upon, they should perform their pantomimes. After each, instruct the audience to briefly describe what they observed. The student may then follow up by reading the portion of his or her sketch that was performed.

Observation Report (166-170)

After writing about personal experiences and the experiences of others, have your students look beyond "people-types" and focus their attention on a particular place in an observation report.

Getting Started: An observation report without good sensory detail is like an oatmeal raisin cookie without the raisins. One of the most important ingredients is missing.

You'll need to do whatever you can to help your students focus on sensory details. One thing you can do is have your students study the sensory detail used in the model observation report (170). You might also try a sensory activity like the following.

Have your students show proper respect for their own senses by listing their most enjoyable sensations: (Encourage them to list as many sensations as they can.)

- ❑ Scent-sation (Identify the smells you like.) Example: Just-baked bread
- ❑ Touch-able (Identify things you like to touch.) Example: Freshly poured cement
- ❑ Taste-ful (Identify the tastes you like.) Example: A tart apple
- ❑ Sight-ly (Identify the sights you like.) Example: Your weekly allowance
- ❑ Sound-er (Identify the sounds you like.) Example: The 3:00 dismissal bell

Enrichment: Instruct your students to hold up their index finger and look very closely at the fingernail. Tell them that the fingernail is a window and they are looking into another world. Have them write an observation report on what they see.

Writing the News Story (171-177)

It seemed like detective Joe Friday in the old *Dragnet* television series was forever saying something like "just the facts, ma'am" to witnesses and suspects he interviewed during investigations. It's "just the facts" that you will want your students to emphasize in their newswriting. And you will want them us use these facts in a special way as outlined in this chapter on writing the news story.

Getting Started: Give your students newswriting practice by having them write a brief, but complete news article about a memorable event in their lives. Also, make sure that you review the writing guidelines and the model story with your students before they start out.

Enrichment: Have groups of students plan and present "Live at 5 (or 8 or 9)" news broadcasts or telecasts.

Writing an Editorial (178-183)

There's probably no skill more difficult for young writers to grasp than developing a persuasive argument. They need as much practice with persuasive writing as you can give them. "Writing an Editorial" is an effective, practical, and productive method of persuasive writing for your students to work with. It's especially productive if your school publishes its own newspaper.

 Helpful HINT Before students develop their own editorials, share a number of models with them. (See 183 and 213 for two examples.) Evaluate these models using the checklist in the handbook as a guide (182).

Getting Started: If your students have trouble selecting a subject suitable for an editorial, try the following activity: Have your students (on their own or in pairs) make a list of "What would happen if...?" statements: "What would happen if the only theater in town closed?" "What would happen if the computer lab were open during the lunch hour?" "What would happen if students had to pass a competency (ability) test before they were allowed to go on to high school?" One of these statements might serve as a starting point for an effective editorial.

Special Points of Interest:

044 "Writing the Personal Essay" (The guidelines in this section provide valuable advice for editorial writers. Editorials are personal essays.)

182 "Correcting: Getting It Right" (Students will find this information helpful when they are evaluating their editorials.)

213 "Letter to an Editor or Official" (The sample letter will serve as a good model editorial for students.)

343 "Thinking Logically" (Logical thinking leads to convincing editorials.)

Enrichment: Have your students break every rule in the book in a "fractured editorial."

Encourage them to assume a new persona for their editorials. On the day that their work is shared, suggest that they dress and act the part of their persona.

If students need rules to break, have them refer to "Fuzzy Thinking," 350, as well as to the regular guidelines in this chapter.

Writing a Summary (184-186)

Why should students write summaries? For two basic reasons. They can write summaries to help themselves make sense out of new concepts and materials presented in their respective classes. In this way, summary writing is an effective writing-to-learn technique. They can also write summaries to indicate to you—their teachers—what they have learned. This is writing to show what they have learned.

As a writing-to-learn technique, students should write summaries as they "think"—in language which is personal, informal, and colloquial. And obviously, when students write summaries to show what they have learned, they should develop their thoughts according to the guidelines established for the assignment or task. Don't assume that your students automatically know how to summarize. As with any form of writing, they can only acquire a real feel for it through regular practice.

Getting Started: After you've discussed the guidelines for summary writing with your students, read aloud "An Invitation to Learning" (001). Instruct students to follow along carefully and, perhaps, list a few main ideas. Then have them review the reading on their own and write a brief summary of this section. Follow with a general discussion of their summaries.

Special Points of Interest:

314 "Understanding Information" (This page discusses the type of thinking that goes on when someone summarizes information.)

361 "Study-Reading Skills" (The techniques for study- reading described in this section are essentially summary techniques.)

421 "The Essay Test" (The guidelines in this section will help students plan and write essay answers for all types of questions—including those questions that ask them to summarize.)

Enrichment: Have pairs of students practice summarizing in the following way: Have each team select a form of writing in *Write Source 2000* to read and learn about. (A page or two of information at a time will do.)

One member reads while the other member becomes an active listener. The listener tells what he or she has heard after the reading. The team then decides together what the essential information is in the reading. Both the reader and listener should write a brief paragraph summarizing what they have learned. These can be compared as well.

Note: This is an effective way for students to get to know their handbooks.

The Book Review (187-191)

An opening word of caution: When you assign book reviews, you are essentially asking your students to evaluate the books they have read. Evaluating is a very advanced level of thinking and writing, and it is not easily mastered. (See 330 for a chart of the different levels of thinking and writing.) So don't expect convincing reviews from young writers. They are only learning to appreciate literature and to think and write about it.

Getting Started: Students really need to become personally engaged in the books they read if you're going to have them write book reviews. That is, they need to explore their personal thoughts and feelings during their reading, so they have a ready supply of ideas and questions to explore when it comes time to develop their book reviews. (To get your students personally engaged in their reading, see pages 64-71 in this booklet.)

Special Points of Interest:

043 "Developing Essays" (Since a review is basically an essay, these guidelines will help students write their book reviews.)

386 "Elements of Literature" (This list of literary terms will give your students a working vocabulary for their reviews.)

327 "Judging Information" (Students will find this discussion of thinking and writing helpful when they develop their reviews.)

Enrichment: Does a book review have to look like your basic essay? We don't think so. We recommend that you give your students a variety of ways to review the books they have read. You might have your students

❑ create bookmarks or posters for the books they read, as if they were a marketing agent trying to sell the book,

❑ write thoughtful letters about the book to the author,

❑ present their thinking about the book to the class (perhaps an oral reading could be worked into their presentation),

❑ or participate in panel discussions about the books that they read.

Writing Letters (192-219)

Students need to write to people outside of the classroom for real reasons. And why? They take their writing more seriously if they know someone "out there" is going to read what they have to say. Letter writing is tailor made for this purpose—especially business letter writing. This section includes guidelines for writing business letters as well as a number of model letters. You will also find guidelines for writing friendly letters.

Getting Started: You might want to ask your students to react to the following question about letter writing: How important is letter writing to you? Consider reading the introductory page on letter writing in *Write Source 2000* (192) before or after you ask this question.

You might also have students brainstorm for situations when a letter would be the best way to communicate. Or you might have them do a little personal research about letter writing. Have them talk to friends, immediate family members, and relatives about letter writing and what it means (or doesn't mean) to them.

Enrichment: (For a business letter) Have students write a "fan" letter along the lines of the model in *Write Source 2000*. (See 195.)

Creative Writing

"Clearly, by the 'creative process,' we mean the capacity to find new and unexpected dimensions, to voyage freely over the seas, to happen on America as we seek new routes to India, to find new relationships in time and space, and thus new meanings."
—Lawrence S. Kubie

Rationale: Creative thinking and writing don't automatically happen as soon as you ask your students to write a poem, a story, or a short play. Creativity is much too temperamental for that. Students must be stimulated and challenged before they will put their imaginations to work. They must be encouraged to take risks and know that it is okay to make mistakes. And they must have the support of their fellow writers and teacher as they develop their work.

It's up to you to make sure that these conditions are met so that creativity feels welcome in your classroom. Then it's up to your students (with the help of this section in their handbook) to shape their creative thinking and writing into effective finished pieces.

Writing Poetry (221-236)

Students only need to give poetry a chance, and they'll find it an enjoyable form of writing to work with—if for no other reason than that it's a change from the type of writing they normally do. The key is to start your students out on the right foot—that is, to make poetry appealing, nonthreatening, and fun . . . right from the start.

Getting Started: Have your students produce a poem right away. Once they realize that they are, in fact, poets in the making, they'll be much more receptive to reading about poetry in their handbooks and writing additional poems.

Here's an easy and almost foolproof way your students can produce an effective little poem. Have them take a close look at your school and record three or four brief scenes that draw their attention. (Tell them to look for things that would make for interesting snapshots.) Have your students write one sentence for each observation.

Now comes the fun part. Tell your students to pull the rug from under one or more of their sentences so that the words spill into a tumble-down poem as in the example which follows:

Sentence: These dusty stairs lead to the attic room where old, forgotten band uniforms lay.

Tumble-Down Poem: These dusty stairs
            lead to the attic room
            where
            old, forgotten
            band uniforms
            lay.

Helpful HINT

It always helps to have plenty of model poems on hand when you have your students write poems. (Make sure that your students take note of the various models in "Writing Poetry.") For many students, models are all they need. Once they see various poems, they have no problem shaping their own creations.

Special Points of Interest:

229 "Reading and Appreciating a Poem" (Take time to read and appreciate a wide variety of poems with your students. The guidelines on this page will help you and your students get the most out of the poems you read.)

230 "An Introduction to Traditional Poetry" (Anything your students will need to know about traditional poetry is included here.)

235 "The Forms of 'Invented' Poetry" (Give your students every opportunity to experiment with a number of these forms.)

331 "Thinking Creatively" (This section will help your students discover new and unexpected ideas for their poems and other creative projects.)

Enrichment: Here's another poetic form you might want to try with your students: Have them preserve some of their random thoughts in a **thought-trap poem**. First, have students identify some object (a book, a purse, a doodle on a folder, etc.) in the first line of their poems. Then ask students to list random thoughts as they come to mind. Encourage them to list ideas nonstop until they feel it is time to trap these thoughts in a poem by repeating the first line.

Story Writing (237-252)

"Whatever you write, no matter how abstract or impersonal it might be, you are always telling some part of your own story. It's impossible to put pen to paper without revealing something about yourself."
—John Rouse

In the first line of "Story Writing" we remind your students that each one of them is a born storyteller. And we really believe that. We vividly remember all of the students in our own classes who loved to tell stories about their personal experiences. Storytelling was natural, enjoyable, and necessary for them—it reaffirmed their special place among their classmates.

We also recognize that the personal stories students are so willing to share serve as a perfect lead into writing fiction. How so? Much of fiction stems from true stories that have simply been rerouted in some way from their original courses. Names may have been changed, incidents may have been altered, conflicts may have been added—but essentially many of the stories your students read are based on real-life situations. This is an important point to keep in mind. Your students already have plenty of raw material to draw from as they begin to write fiction. They just need practice "reshaping" their own stories into effective finished pieces. The advice and guidelines in "Story Writing" will help them meet this end.

Getting Started: Have students in pairs share surprising, amusing, and important personal experiences. Afterwards, ask for volunteers to share their stories with the class. Select one of the stories to analyze. That is, as a class, identify the main parts of the story: the characters, the setting, the main activity, and the conflict. Have students do the same for one of their own stories. Then, help students fictionalize their stories by altering one or more of the main parts.

Where do you go from here? After reviewing the guidelines for story writing in the handbook, why not have students develop their altered personal stories into pieces of fiction?

Special Points of Interest:

239 "Inventing Stories: A How-to Interview with a Real Story Writer" (This interview provides plenty of practical advice plus plenty of laughs.)

244 "Connecting: Taking Inventory of Your Story" (This checklist will help your students evaluate their work in progress.)

253 "Writing Dialogue" (Stories need dialogue. This chapter answers any questions students may have about writing dialogue.)

Enrichment: Have your students individually or in pairs plan a popular short story. Suggest that students choose from the story types described in the short story sampler (247). A simple plan for students to follow is provided in the interview in this chapter (see 239).

A Special Challenge: Have them develop their plans into award-winning stories to share with their classmates.

Writing Dialogue (253-256)

What language arts teacher isn't frustrated by the way many students use or misuse dialogue in their writing? Either it sounds too stiff and unnatural, it ends too abruptly or continues on much too long, or it is "punctuated" in a way that makes it almost impossible to follow. "Writing Dialogue" won't remake your students into skilled writers of discourse; only plenty of practice and guidance will do that. But this brief chapter does provide plenty of practical advice that will at least point your student writers in the right direction.

Getting Started: Have your students complete "Road Trip," a minilesson on writing dialogue. (See page 107 in this booklet.)
Note: Make sure you share examples of effectively written dialogue and discuss this chapter with your students before they work on this minilesson.

Special Point of Interest:
511 "Quotation Marks" (When students have questions about punctuating dialogue, this is where they should turn in their handbooks.)

Enrichment: Review "Imaginary Conversations" (254) with your class. Then have them develop imaginary conversations of their own. They can use the prompt given in the handbook or come up with one of their own. Remind them to refer to "The Yellow Pages" for help with punctuating.

A Special Challenge: Have your students continue the conversation started in the sample dialogue (256).

 See the "Minilessons" section (pages 93-110) for additional activities.

Writing Plays (257-263)

> "*. . . plays represent the least abstracted, most detailed rendering of a story possible. Students who have had experience scripting tend, when writing regular narrative, to have a better sense of how much detail is required and when to include or exclude it.*"
> —James Moffett and Betty Jane Wagner

A story is a story—whether it is played out in narrative form or "acted out" by a set of interesting characters in a play. As a result, the way you and your students approach play or script writing should not be a great deal different from the way you approach story writing. It's best to begin with the students' own experiences and help them reshape these experiences into basic dramatic forms. We suggest that you begin with basic scripts, maybe something as basic as brief invented dialogues, and move slowly and carefully to more lengthy scripts with larger casts of characters and more complex conflicts.

If your students have already completed the suggested activities in "Writing Dialogue," they've already worked with very basic script forms. If not, have them work through that brief chapter and the suggested activities before tackling "Writing Plays."

Getting Started: Start right in with a "theater in the round" script-writing session. Here's how: Have your students form into groups of five or six script writers. Then distribute the first few lines of a script to each group. Use the sample script in the handbook (260) if you want, or make up your own.

Then have your students add a line (and perhaps a new character) when the script comes their way. Encourage students to keep the script moving as quickly as possible. Spontaneity is important. When you feel students have had enough, stop the round robin writing and have one person from each group read their finished product. Students will have fun with this activity. And you might find elements in each of the scripts that deserve to be discussed as you formally introduce "Writing Plays" to your class.

Enrichment: Have students individually or in pairs plan a short play using the "Sample Collection Sheet" (259) as their guide.
Note: It's okay if they can't complete every last detail on this sheet.

A Special Challenge: Have the playwrights put their plans into script form following the guidelines in their handbooks. Encourage your drama freaks to stage their plays.

"Research writing is one of the most complex intellectual activities we ask students to undertake. We are, in effect, asking them to perform the tasks of a scholar en route to publication."
—Wisconsin Department of Public Instruction

Searching to Learn

Rationale: How can you make sure that your students really get engaged in research and report projects? First of all, you must make sure that the entire research process is as lively and active as you can make it. Encourage your students to select research topics that they have a genuine interest in, bring in guest speakers, let your students collaborate on research projects, and so on.

Also, ask your students to gather information from a variety of resources, encourage them to conduct some firsthand research, and make sure they put as much or more effort into developing their thoughts as they do into developing the form of their papers or reports. If you establish these general guidelines for your students, they can't help but approach research and report projects with enthusiasm. The guidelines in "Searching to Learn" will help your students put this enthusiasm to good use when they develop their personal research papers and their classroom reports.

Chapter Summaries

Personal Research and Writing (265-270)

What better reason is there for anyone—young learners, teachers, scholars, thoughtful consumers—to engage in research than to answer a pressing question, to satisfy one's curiosity, to basically set out on a personal quest for information? Put another way, what other reason can there be? We can't think of any, especially when it comes to young learners. "Personal Research and Writing" is designed to engage your students in the type of meaningful research just described. We help students select research topics that are of genuine interest to them on a very personal level, we help them conduct their research, and finally, we help them share the results of their researching adventure in an engaging fashion.

Getting Started: If your students have trouble selecting a research subject, have them generate ideas as described in the writing tip (see 268).

Helpful HINT You can find any number of personal research projects to use as models in newspapers and magazines. Many feature articles in periodicals tell the story of the writer's quest for information.

Enrichment: After students have experienced a personal research project, challenge them later in the year to develop an engaging personal research story out of a very general subject. Give them a list of topics including apples, cats, flies, stars, cars, trees, and so on, and see what they can make out of one of these.

The Classroom Report (271-286)

There's an up side and a down side to assigning reports. First the up side: Reports can give students practice working with a variety of resources, compiling and organizing information, and developing lengthy pieces of writing.

Now the down side: The starting point for most report assignments is usually a list of teacher-imposed topics, which means students have little freedom to choose a specific subject to research and write about. Also, students often rely on encyclopedias (and other oversized reference books) to compile their reports. And, not surprisingly, their finished products resemble the encyclopedia articles they read. And, more often than not, students find it hard to budget their time for an extended project like a report, especially if they are doing much of the work on their own, outside of class.

Keep these points in mind when your students develop their classroom reports. We feel it's especially important that you encourage your students to write about something that interests them, that they refer to a variety of resources during their research, and that you help them budget their time during the entire research and writing process. Also, make sure that your students refer to "The Classroom Report" for researching and writing advice, step-by-step guidelines, and the model report.

Getting Started: Have students search for possible report topics in the following way: Ask them to do some preliminary research for three possible topics. For each topic, have them identify three interesting things they have learned during their initial research and three different sources they could use to find out more about this topic. From this preliminary research, they can choose a topic for their report.

In 273 we suggest that students write some basic questions that they would like to answer in their reports. If your students have trouble developing these questions, writers Susan and Steven Tchudi suggest that they try question clusters—rapidly recording questions (rather than words) that come to mind when they think of their report subject, the nucleus word of the cluster. (See 035 for an explanation of clustering.)

Special Points of Interest:

280 "Giving Credit for Information Used in a Report" (If you expect your students to give credit in their reports, make sure that you discuss this information with them.)

284 "Model Report" (Encourage students to refer to the model to see firsthand how credit is given in a report and works are cited in a bibliography.)

Enrichment: Have your students put their research and report-writing experience to good use by making your classroom the research and resource center for your school, the school system, and the community. Have teachers, students, and community members submit questions they want answered, information they want compiled, and references they want checked. Then have students (preferably in teams) search for answers and information and develop their findings into mini-reports.

Computers and Writing (287-289)

More and more of your students have personal computers and more and more of your schools are equipped with computer writing labs—which means that more and more of your young writers will want to prepare their writing assignments on computers. What does this mean for you? You must have some firsthand experience composing with a computer and some knowledge of the various word processing programs on the market, so you can answer questions your students may have as they come on-line. Our discussion in this brief chapter provides a good introduction for writers just getting into computers.

Getting Started: If you have access to a computer lab, have your students prepare a brief piece of writing on a computer from start to finish. Then have them list the pluses and minuses of composing with a computer. Make this list the focus of a discussion on computers and writing. Also, read and react to "Computers and Writing" in *Write Source 2000* during this discussion.

Special Point of Interest:

839-847 "Using the Computer" (Basic computer terms and commands are listed here. Also included is a sample computer keyboard with the home row highlighted.)

Enrichment: Encourage students to practice keyboarding as often as they can. Provide some incentive for practicing—perhaps a certain number of bonus points for 15-30 minutes of practice time. (Of course, this is only fair if everyone has access to a computer.)

Using the Library (290-304)

This section focuses on the basic information students need in order to use the library: how to use the card catalog, what's included in the reference section (besides the encyclopedias), and how to use the *Readers' Guide*, the thesaurus, and the dictionary. It's up to you and your librarian to point out other types of information and services most libraries have to offer.

Getting Started: Before or after a general discussion of the library, have each student submit a question that they want answered. Something on the order of "How long do mosquitoes live," not "What is the last word in the third paragraph in chapter fourteen in *Huckleberry Finn?*" "What country has the highest per capita income," not "What is the most interesting article in the most recent issue of *Road & Track* magazine?" Students then pick a question out of a hat to answer, using the resources in the school library. They should present to the class not only an answer (or nonanswer, if that is the case) but also the story of their search: "First I did . . ., then I looked in . . ., and finally I. . . ."

Enrichment: If at all possible, have your school, community, or university librarian discuss with your students the influence of technology on library services. There are a lot of fascinating things happening in today's libraries because of technology. Your students should be made aware of these latest advances.

Note: A field trip to a "hi-tech" library would be well worth the effort.

Thinking to Learn

Rationale: The opening to "Teaching Thinking in the '90s" (page 83 in this booklet) discusses in detail why a section in our handbook is devoted to thinking. We make note in that discussion that teachers should teach **for thinking** by creating the right classroom climate, **about thinking** by helping students become more aware of their own thinking, and **of thinking** by teaching thinking skills. Creating the right classroom climate for the teaching of thinking skills is your responsibility. (You'll find plenty of suggestions in "Teaching Thinking in the '90s" to meet these ends.)

In "Thinking to Learn" we've taken on a lot of the responsibility ourselves to help your students become more aware of their own thinking. We identify, among other things, steps students can take to think more carefully, how various levels of thinking apply to the writing they do, and how they can think more creatively and logically.

> *"There are one-story intellects, two-story intellects, and three-story intellects with skylights. All fact collectors who have no aim beyond their facts are one-story men. Two-story men compare, reason, generalize, using the labor of fact collectors as their own. Three-story men idealize, imagine, predict—their best illumination comes from above the skylight."*
> —Oliver Wendell Holmes

Chapter Summaries
Thinking Better (306-310)

If students are going to improve as thinkers—that is, think more carefully and "thoughtfully"—they should become more aware of their own thinking process. (You might be familiar with the term metacognition. It is a professional buzzword that refers to thinking about thinking.) "Thinking Better" provides an excellent introduction to the fine art of "metacogitating." (The section on thinking in this booklet suggests a number of ways you can help your students metacogitate.)

Getting Started: Before you have your students read and react to "The Planet of Bad Thinkers," have them create and briefly describe (one paragraph) their own group of bad thinkers—perhaps a class-room of bad thinkers, a team of bad thinkers, a game show for bad thinkers, a ship of fools, and so on. Have them list characteristics of their bad thinkers. Perhaps they never read the directions for any assignment, they let the strongest and best hitter bat first, or they yell out answers before they really know the complete question.

Enrichment: Refer to the last two pages in the thinking section "Using Your Brain." Talk about the brain: how it works, the whole left brain/right brain issue, the different thinking phases we go through. If at all possible, team up with a science teacher, a local doctor, or a brain specialist and make this a real "whole brain" activity.

Note: Check your school or local library for videotapes of special public television programs on the brain.

Thinking and Writing (311-330)

Carnegie Foundation President Ernest Boyer has stated, "Clear writing leads to clear thinking; clear thinking is the basis of clear writing." He, along with any number of individuals connected with education, recognizes the special interrelationship between clear thinking and effective writing. You can't have one without the other. To help your students grow as thinkers and writers, consider implementing writing activities which gradually increase in reasoning complexity and discuss the level(s) of reasoning or thinking required for each activity.

If this is too prescriptive for you, at least be aware of the type of thinking involved in each type of writing activity you assign and make sure your students are aware of this as well. For many writing activities, it's not enough to let students know *what* they are supposed to do. You should also let them know *how* they are supposed to carry out the activity by helping them understand the type of thinking involved. However you address the writing/thinking connection with your students, you will find this chapter helpful.

Getting Started: Have students briefly describe the most challenging thinking tasks they have ever performed. Perhaps one student memorized a lengthy list of difficult terms. Another student may have helped design the perfect tree house for his little brother, and still another student may have organized and classified a cardboard box full of family photographs. Use this activity as a lead-in to a discussion of the different levels of thinking. (Refer to "Thinking About Questions and Answers," 330, during your discussion. It provides a taxonomy of thinking skills.)

Special Points of Interest:

310 "Your Basic Writing and Thinking Moves" (This chart will help your students make the right thinking moves as they plan more complex pieces of writing.)

330 "Thinking About Questions and Answers" (In addition to providing you and your students with a taxonomy of thinking terms, this chart helps students understand what is being asked of them when they are instructed to *define, summarize, classify,* and so on.)

Enrichment: If you have students write in journals, periodically provide them with writing prompts which promote certain levels of thinking—especially those levels of thinking you want to emphasize throughout the school year. For example, a prompt like "A classmate I will never forget" emphasizes basic *recall* and *understanding.* A prompt like "What if I never forgot" emphasizes *speculating*, a more complex level of thinking.

Thinking Creatively (331-342)

How can you promote creative thinking and writing in your classroom? First of all, plan classroom activities which promote creative thinking skills like fluency, flexibility, elaboration, and originality. And secondly, encourage your students to think open-endedly and to take risks in your classroom. A creative thinker is not a one-way thinker always looking for right answers. "Thinking Creatively" describes the creative mind in action and works well as an introduction to creative thinking and writing.

Getting Started: To promote open-ended and original thinking, have your students focus on one (or more) of the questions asked in "What if . . . ?" (334) and generate as many answers as they can.
A variation: Have pairs of students alternate answers and work from each other's creative thinking. Have them write rapidly and spontaneously.

Enrichment: Have your students complete the minilesson "Can't See the Monkeys from the Bus." (See page 108 in this booklet.) This lesson will really get them thinking and writing creatively.

Thinking Logically (343-355)

Who is a good thinker? According to Allan A. Glatthorn and Jonathan Baron (in *Developing Minds*), a good thinker is someone who welcomes problematic situations and is tolerant of ambiguity. A good thinker is someone who is reflective and deliberative, some-one who believes in the value and the power of logic. And a good thinker is someone who searches and researches until he or she is satisfied that a goal has been reached, a question has been answered, a fact has been verified.

This is all pretty heady stuff, especially when you think in terms of your students. But they are all potentially "good thinkers," and, in their own way and to the best of their ability, will become so with the proper guidance and experience. This chapter provides you and your students with a good introduction to the process of logical thinking and also provides your students with an excellent guide for writing clearly, logically, and persuasively.

Getting Started: Have some "good thinkers"—maybe a panel of good thinkers—speak to your class. Perhaps you could have a local attorney describe how he or she prepares and presents a convincing case. A physician could describe how she makes a diagnosis, prepares and carries out an operation, and proposes a plan for recovery. A car mechanic could describe what it means to "troubleshoot" and share some challenging car problems he has dealt with. A builder could describe the step-by-step approach he takes to construct a house. A coach could describe how he or she plans a strategy for an upcoming opponent, and so on.

Special Points of Interest:

344-349 "Guidelines for Persuasive Writing and Thinking" (These guidelines will help students form opinion statements and support them with clear, provable facts.)

350-355 "Avoid Fuzzy Thinking" (Young learners are all too ready to jump to conclusions, exaggerate facts, and express ideas which contain half-truths. The advice and examples in this section may help them see the shortcomings or "fuzziness" of this type of thinking.)

Enrichment: Have pairs or small groups of students stage debates, discussions, or old-fashioned arguments which focus on topical and controversial issues. (During the give and take of ideas, the distinctive personality of each debater should become apparent.)

The rest of the class should evaluate the debaters' performance. Have them pay special attention to the strength of each debater's argument. (Refer them to 344-355 for guidelines.)

Reading to Learn

Rationale: When students are asked to read to learn, they are obligated to tackle unfamiliar subjects, different kinds of texts, and a wide spectrum of supplemental materials.

Therefore, this section has been included to help students meet these reading challenges, to discover strategies to aid their reading comprehension, and to help them remember information.

The four reading-to-learn strategies presented in the first chapter, plus the vocabulary-building techniques also included in this section, will help students become independent learners. Once they have received instruction and guided practice, they can use these strategies without your help and study-read more effectively.

> ***"Reading is to the mind what exercise is to the body."***
> ***—Richard Steele***

Chapter Summaries
Study-Reading Skills (361-370)

KWL (listing what a reader already KNOWS about a particular topic, discovering what the reader WANTS to learn, and finally listing what the reader has LEARNED) is a simple yet effective study-reading strategy. It can be used as a prereading activity to create anticipation by asking students to complete the "K" and "W" columns. It becomes an encouraging wrap-up for a unit when students complete the "L" column.

The next two strategies, mapping (364) and word pictures (365), are very popular with middle school learners. **Mapping** (sometimes called mind maps or webs) can be used before, during, or after students read. It helps them organize content, formulate concepts, and focus on the key words. It helps students distinguish between the main point and supporting details. Building a map while you and your students brainstorm about an upcoming unit or reading material helps you assess what your students already know and gives you the advantage of building on their prior knowledge.

Mapping can be very creative. Pictures, phrases, shapes, colors, and actual objects (leaves, acorns, bark) can be used as well as words.

Word pictures are graphic organizers which help students reconstruct their textbook reading. Word pictures are effective ways for middle school students

to take notes because they help students overcome two common difficulties: deciding what to include and how to organize it. (See topic numbers 413-417 for additional information about note taking.)

Although the **SQ3R** method (366) may look complex since it occupies a full page, mature, gifted, or highly motivated readers often rely on SQ3R more than any other study-reading method. It shows students that reading to learn is a process and includes one of the most powerful ways to comprehend: verbalizing.

Helpful HINT To build interest in SQ3R, we suggest that students make note cards, flash cards, and illustrations as the final step in the process. Sharing note cards (different groups might be responsible for different portions of a chapter) or using flash cards works especially well when reviewing.

The guidelines for reading to learn(367-369) provide valuable commonsense tips. Teachers in all content areas can direct their students to this page at the beginning of the year to help them develop personal learning plans. When you ask students to evaluate their performance at the end of a unit or semester, this page can serve as a guide to help them discover what they are doing well and what they could do better.

Getting Started: To help students experience these personal reading and learning tools, introduce a new strategy or particular word picture each week. Ask them to use these strategies as often as possible throughout the day. Hold desk-side conferences to provide students with feedback which will help them refine their work. Comparing their results in small groups is another way to reinforce how effectively these strategies are working for students.

Enrichment: Ask students to create a "How to Learn" booklet, describing and illustrating methods of learning they have found effective. These booklets could be shared with other classrooms or younger students. Students could visit other classrooms and show students firsthand how to use one (or more) of the learning techniques they have found helpful.

Improving Vocabulary (370-384)

Using context clues (370), which students often regard as time-consuming and boring, takes on new life here. Students discover there are seven ways to unravel a mysterious word. Becoming a sleuth, a detective, or a private eye appeals to middle school students.

Getting Started: Unlocking unfamiliar vocabulary words in pairs or small groups becomes a game when students use context clues. Simply supply students with passages which contain these words and let them try to figure out their meaning using the context clues described in their handbooks (370). Ask one group member to report their "findings" to the class.

Enrichment: Instead of writing definitions for words, students might compose sentences which "reveal" the words in context.

Note: When context clues are not sufficient, students should be advised to turn the page and use additional tools to unlock the meaning of words: a dictionary, thesaurus, or word parts.

Prefixes, Suffixes, and Roots (374-384)

Word parts—prefixes (374-376), suffixes (377), and roots (378-384)—are invaluable bits of information, but your students may not see it this way. Telling them that these little bits of information will help them build an impressive vocabulary may not do much good either. You will have to show them—that is, actually put these word parts to use in activities—before they will appreciate their value. (See pages 89-90 in this booklet for ideas.)

Kinds of Literature and Elements of Literature (385-387)

The general kinds of literature as well as any of the elements your students may need to know are included in these two lists. Make a master list of literary types and terms you want your students to know; then refer them to the two lists for definitions and examples.

Note: These lists can be helpful both when students are reading or studying literature and when they are writing or presenting book reviews.

Speaking and Listening to Learn

Rationale: Speaking is language in action, language played out in its most natural state. It is the one aspect of language in which your students are most at ease, most confident, most capable (unless, of course, they're speaking in foreign territory like your classroom). As the old saying goes: "We gotta talk." We applaud you if speaking is an important part of your language arts program. You know how it can motivate your students, enliven your classroom, and enhance learning. You also know that it is just as important, perhaps even more important than the study of writing and reading and grammar. We encourage the rest of you to give speaking more playing time in your classes, and not just in late inning relief appearances either. Put it right in your starting rotation. Speaking is much too valuable to play a secondary role.

Your students will find "Speaking and Listening to Learn" especially helpful when they develop formal speeches, oral readings, and conduct interviews. Also included are guidelines for speaking's battery mate—listening.

> *"I believe that every child begins with the drive to explore the world he is born into, that curiosity is indeed 'native.' Speech becomes its principal instrument."*
> —James Britton

Chapter Summaries
Preparing a Speech (389-398)

Mark Twain once said, "It usually takes me more than three weeks to prepare a good impromptu speech." In his classic tongue-in-cheek style, Twain is telling us that for most occasions speaking is much more than standing on a soapbox and ad-libbing. Speaking is thinking and writing and rehearsing and then presenting. That's how we approach preparing a speech in this chapter—as a deliberate process which involves a good deal of planning and preparation. Your students will find the advice, guidelines, and helpful hints easy to follow and effective.

Getting Started: Here is an effective warm-up activity. Have students interview someone in the class that they don't know very well. Encourage them to be creative in the types of questions they ask: What three things have you never done? What will be your address in 20 years? Or what secret something don't we know about you?

Using the guidelines in this chapter, each student should then develop a brief introductory speech to present to the class. Point out that the manner in which they "introduce" their subjects is up to them. They may want to develop a campaign speech, make a toast, file charges, etc.

 Remind your students that whenever one student is speaking, the rest of the class should be listening. Refer them to the listening skills (402) whenever you feel it is appropriate.

Enrichment: Have your students observe and evaluate experienced speakers in action. (Use videotapes of speakers if in-person observations are impossible.) Review the speaking (398) and listening guidelines (402) with your students before the speech presentation. You might want to develop a critique sheet for them as well.

Note: Make every effort to have speakers visit your classroom. There are any number of individuals in every community willing to contribute their time and effort if you just ask them.

Reading to Others (400-401)

When actors and actresses audition for a part, they often are given a script to rehearse and read. They prepare for their audition in much the same way your students should prepare for an oral reading. They read their lines again and again in private until they feel they really know the script. They ask themselves if they want to speak fast or slow or a combination of speeds, if they want to speak loudly or softly, if they want to emphasize certain words, and so on. They want to make sure that they make a good impression during their audition. Make this connection for your students, and they might look at oral reading in a new light . . . with more enthusiasm. Then share with them the guidelines in "Reading to Others" before they get to work on their own scripts.

Getting Started: Make a variety of possible reading selections available to your students. Get your librarian to help you. Consider short plays, poems, song lyrics, dramatic excerpts from short stories and novels, newspaper and magazine articles, letters, diaries, etc. Remind students to select a script that would interest them if they were on the other end—that is, if they were the listener.

Enrichment: Have your students prepare oral readings for a specific audience—younger elementary students, the PTA, the student body of your school, a senior citizen's group, etc.

Interviewing (405-407)

We feel that it's important for you to break down the walls of your classroom, so to speak, and help your students see the connection between what they are doing in school and what goes on in the real world. That's why we encourage students to write regularly in a personal journal, to write letters for information, to conduct personal research projects. And that's why we've included a brief chapter on "Interviewing." It is one more way—a very effective way—for students to make contact "with the outside."

Getting Started: Students need to see and hear an effective interview in action, so give them one. That is, "stage" an interview for them. Perhaps you could be the subject of the interview, and a fellow teacher could be the interviewer. Or you could work with a pair of students willing to stage an interview for you. Videotape the interview and use it as part of a discussion on the art of interviewing.

Note: It would also be great to get a local news reporter into your classroom to share his or her interviewing experiences.

Enrichment: Use the minilesson "Mind if I tape this?" (see page 108 in this booklet) to give everyone some firsthand interviewing experience before they interview someone outside of school.

Learning to Learn

Rationale: There are four general learning areas (*classroom skills, taking tests, group skills,* and *individual skills*) which offer teachers of every discipline an opportunity to help students develop the skills they need to become more efficient learners. One of the best **classroom skills** to get students thinking in science, math, history — in any class—is to write in learning logs. If you are using collaborative learning or thinking about using it, you will appreciate our discussion of **groups skills**. Also, students need to be shown —and reshown— how to **take tests**. This information will increase their chances for success by encouraging them to prepare sooner and more carefully. Because research has proven that students need a safe environment (a place where they will take learning risks and nurture self-esteem) educators have an even greater appreciation for **individual skills**, among them setting goals, managing time, and managing stress. By using this section of the handbook, you can help students develop the individual skills, interests, and attitudes they will need for the lifelong pursuit of learning.

Chapter Summaries

Classroom Skills (409-417)

Keeping a **learning log** is one of the best classroom activities for enhancing learning.

Getting Started:
Step 1: Explain to students that learning logs are a place for them to think . . . an academic log. They will become mathematicians, historians, scientists, and researchers when they work in their learning logs. They will explore their thoughts to discover more about the data, processes, events, people, and concepts they meet in their texts. They will include opinions, attitudes, insights, and questions.

Step 2: Each day for the first week or two, show students a technique they can use in their academic logs. (See pages 78-80 in this booklet; also, refer students to topic numbers 412-417 in their handbooks.) Choose techniques which students will find most useful in the discipline you are teaching. The following is a sample of general techniques that will work in most classes:

Day 1: KWL (topic 363)

Day 2: Compare and Contrast Word Picture (topic 365)

Day 3: Listing (page 80 in this booklet)

Day 4: Mapping (topic 364)

Day 5: Focused Writings (page 79 in this booklet)

Step 3: You can also provide an occasional "prompt." ("What if. . ." and "Why" questions serve well as prompts.) Sometimes you may want to use a more specific question, especially if students are learning a system or process they will need again and again. Here are some examples of specific prompts: (1) Describe how you think some insects become butterflies. (2) Brainstorm to compile a list of words concerning ancient Rome and Greece. (3) Pretend you are crossing the Potomac with George Washington. Write an entry in your log as if you were one of the soldiers in the boat. (4) We'll be taking an imaginary trip to Venezuela. List at least five questions you would like to find answers to while you are there. (5) If you could stand on Mars, what do you think you would see? (You will also find a list of excellent prompts in *Coming to Know,* Appendix B, "Prompts for Learning Log Entries," Heinemann Educational Books, Inc.)

Step 4: Ask students to write at different times: the beginning of class, the end, and various points in between.

Step 5: Use one of the following methods to share thoughts:

■ Ask each student to read his/her journal entry in a small group. Group members can make comments, discuss, and ask questions.

■ Quickly go around the room, letting each student read his/her entry.

■ Publish a list of comments from student entries and give each student a copy.

Learning logs (academic journals) are most often spiral-bound notebooks where students are asked to list, free-write, chart, create word pictures, observe, speculate, map, brainstorm, ask questions, role-play, activate prior knowledge, compose a wish list, summarize, paraphrase, predict, connect, create new insights, pose theories, write a letter to a teacher, and so on. Learning logs help students become more active learners. They help teachers break away from the lecture-listen pattern and give each student a classroom voice.

Learning logs should not be graded or corrected. However, the entries are counted. Every student must write, and sharing entries is especially productive. Students will be very curious about what other students are thinking. They will gather more data, hear different interpretations, and expand their knowledge when they listen to what classmates write.

Enrichment: Suggest related activities, topics, or prompts to stimulate critical thinking in their learning journal, a convenient "workplace" which students can turn to at home or whenever time permits:

❑ Write a poem using some of the information in the text or your learning log.

❑ What songs do you think George Washington liked? Why?

❑ If you had to convert this information into a book for younger children, what would you include? How would you help them understand? Would you use illustrations? Charts?

❑ How many ways did you use water today?

> ***"On this October morning I asked them to open their new journals to the first page where, as usual, they entered the date and time. Then I directed them: 'Think about and list as many different, unusual ways that we might write in math.'"***
> —Anne Thompson

Taking Tests (418-431)

Taking tests is another way to learn (and not just a way to show what has already been learned). This attitude helps both instructors and students use testing wisely. As more and more educators use whole language and performance-based learning, testing is becoming an important avenue for discovering meaning. Such an attitude is the opposite of telling some students they learned the material in exactly the right way (A+) and telling other students they didn't learn anything (F).

There should always be time after testing to help every student relearn everything he/she missed. When students have mastered the content, they can help other students, locate and read supplemental materials, or do enrichment activities. These choices will offer valuable practice time for interactive and oral skills, locating information, and becoming independent learners.

Getting Started: Using the guidelines found at topic numbers 428-431, ask students to WRITE 5-10 objective questions. These questions can form the basis for review or be used in an actual test. Students can do the same for essay tests using the key words found at topic numbers 422 and 423.

Enrichment: Ask another teacher to loan you some essay tests he/she has used in the past. Let your students practice their test-taking skills and meet in small groups to discuss which answers or parts of answers best complete the questions.

Group Skills (432-449)

Any classroom will function better if you encourage your students to use group skills. As teachers, we have become more and more aware that (1) students can learn from each other, (2) that employers want people who know and practice group skills, and (3) that making our classrooms mentally and emotionally safe places for our students increases their chances of learning. Insisting that students practice groups skills makes these three objectives possible.

Getting Started: Read independently or as a class the information in topic numbers 439-441, "Skills for Cooperating." Next, form small groups and ask students to share entries from their learning logs. While they share and discuss, ask them to practice these three skills. Afterwards, you may ask them to make a learning log entry about their small group experiences and how they feel about these three skills.

Enrichment: The people skills listed in this section of the handbook, as well as many others, can be identified in literature and history. Ask students to watch for people using group skills well and not so well. Who encounters greater conflicts because of poor people skills? Who uses people skills to make others feel better and resolve conflicts?

Individual Skills (450-457)

On one of the first days of class, you can let your students know you care about them not only as learners but as people by introducing them to this section of the handbook. By letting your students know you care, you create a safer environment for them and you make it easier for them to relax and pursue learning.

Getting Started with Time Management: Ask your students to create a weekly planner in their learning log and record data for one week. Using this data they can then create a "personal" weekly planner for the remainder of the year.

Getting Started with Stress Management: Ask students to make a journal entry about their personal stress. They should consider causes, symptoms, and ways to realistically reduce some of their stress.

Enrichment: Ask students to locate and read more articles and books about time and/or stress management.

The Yellow Pages

"If there is one conclusion to be drawn which cuts across all the studies, it is this: the more time spent analyzing grammar as grammar, the less time spent writing; the less time spent writing, the less improvement in the written product."
—Sara D'Eloia

Rationale: You will note that we've placed "The Yellow Pages" near the end of the handbook—after all of the guidelines for writing and learning. We did this to emphasize the fact that writing and language learning don't (and shouldn't) begin with the study of grammar. *Remember:* The conventions of our language take on real meaning when students are ready to **share** what they have learned.

You will also note that "The Yellow Pages" are color coded, so it will be easy for your students to flip to this section when they have a question about mechanics, usage, spelling, or grammar. We want your students to run their fingers through this section often and enjoy doing so.

Special Note: Study after study has shown that grammar instruction has little or no bearing on a student's ability to communicate effectively. Students learn to communicate by writing and speaking on a regular basis—not by memorizing grammatical rules and labeling isolated sentences.

Our intention here is not to downplay the importance of grammar. We know as well as you do that your students must have an appreciation of the standard conventions of our language. However, we do suggest that you put the study of grammar in proper perspective and not make it the focus of your writing program. Instead, link it as much as possible to the students' own writing, primarily when they are preparing their work for publication.

Helpful HINT

Make sure you have a good feel for "The Yellow Pages" yourself before you talk about it with your students. There is a great deal of information in this section.

Getting Started and Enrichment: See "What About Grammar?" in this booklet for alternative approaches to grammar instruction. Also, see pages 94-100 for minilessons that go along with "The Yellow Pages."

The Student Almanac

Rationale: We want your students to use *Write Source 2000* in all of their classes as a guide for their writing and learning. But we also want your students to think of the handbook as a general, all-school reference book. That's why we've developed "The Student Almanac." Students will find the many tables, maps, and historical documents helpful in their math, science, geography, and social studies classes.

Getting Started: Have students list all of their classes across the top or along the side of a piece of notebook paper. Then, have them identify parts of "The Student Almanac" that will help them in each of their classes. Also, ask them to identify other parts of the handbook that will help them across the curriculum. (This is an excellent way for students to get to know their handbooks.)

Enrichment: Use "The Student Almanac" as a starting point for "cultural literacy" minilessons. Find one of the many lists detailing what literate Americans need to know. Select people, places, and ideas from such a list in "The Student Almanac" or elsewhere in *Write Source 2000*. Form questions (like those below) that students answer using their handbooks: Where is Puerto Rico? What is a centimeter? What does the Preamble to the Constitution mean to you? When did the Panama Canal open? Proceed from there with a discussion of the questions and the students' answers.

Helpful HINT

Special Note: Make sure that teachers in all disciplines are aware of all of the valuable information in *Write Source 2000*. And encourage all teachers to make use of the handbook with their students. *Write Source 2000* improves with use. That is, the more students use it, the more they will value it as a helpful learning tool.

"If we succeed in giving the love of learning, the learning itself is sure to follow."
—John Lubbock

Getting Started

The pages which follow

can be used to introduce *WS 2000*

to your students and get them started

on the road to becoming

active, independent learners.

Using *Write Source 2000:*
Getting Started Activities

The *Write Source 2000* handbook was written by teachers for students. More than anything else, the teachers wanted to put together a handbook that students would like and actually use. Over the past several years, both students and teachers have told us what they like best about the handbook, what they would like to see added or changed, and what they do when the book is first put into the hands of the students. Here are some of the suggestions they sent us:

What would you put in a handbook?

Before you even hand out *Write Source 2000,* ask students what they would put into an all-purpose student handbook if they were in charge of designing one. We have included an activity sheet to help your students design their handbooks. (See "You Have Been Called.") We also have included a follow-up activity which asks students to compare and contrast the handbook they designed with our handbook.

Scavenger Hunts

Another popular idea with both students and teachers is the scavenger hunt. Ask your students to find a random list of items in *Write Source 2000.* (Some should be fairly obvious, some less so.) Create your own lists of items for your students to find or use one of the scavenger hunts we have provided for you (Scavenger Hunts A or B).

■ A variation on the scavenger hunt is the "Getting to Know My Handbook" activity. Challenge your students to find suitable words from *Write Source 2000* to fill in the "Getting to Know" chart. The words they choose must begin with the letters in "Write Source."

■ Another Variation: Ask students to find one, two, three, or more items in *Write Source 2000* which are interesting and valuable to know, but which are not necessarily obvious or easy to locate. Students can then challenge the class to find these items.

■ Still Another Variation: Duplicate and distribute copies of "Easy Liftoff" for an enjoyable and fast-paced handbook search. You might make a contest out of this activity and see who can get the most correct answers in a specified amount of time.

Other Activities

■ Give your students the following assignment: Find one page, one short section, one set of guidelines, one illustration, one model, one important fact, or one quotation you find interesting, entertaining, stimulating, valuable, etc. Students should prepare to share their discoveries with members of their discussion group or with the entire class.

■ Give your students ten minutes to page through *Write Source 2000.* Have students then develop a cluster with *Write Source 2000* as the nucleus word. (See 035 in the handbook for an explanation of clustering.) Or, have them write freely for 5 or 10 minutes (the focus of this writing should be their first impressions). Discuss the results of their clustering or writing.

■ Have students develop *who, what, when, where, why,* and *how* questions from *Write Source 2000.* Students should then exchange questions with a partner and search for answers in the handbook. Upon completion, partners should read and react to each other's answers.

Example questions:

Who would make an interesting figure for a character sketch?

What is the first step in the writing process?

Special Challenge: Develop questions which teams of students try to answer using the handbook. Pattern this activity after a popular game show.

Using *Write Source 2000*:
Your First Week with the Handbook

The following sequence of activities will help you and your students get to know *Write Source 2000*. (Adjust accordingly.)

DAY 1 Duplicate and distribute "You Have Been Called." Have your students work on this activity on their own or in pairs. Help students with the first question: What would you put in a student handbook? Generate ideas as a class, and list them.

DAY 2 Provide time at the beginning of the class period for students to complete their handbook planning. When they complete this activity, have students share their design ideas. Discuss the results of their planning as a class.

Pass out individual copies of *Write Source 2000*. Give students sufficient time to review their handbooks. If time permits, have them share first impressions. Otherwise, do that during the next class period.

For an assignment, have students complete "Compare and Contrast"—an activity sheet we've provided for you.

DAY 3 Discuss the comparisons and contrasts between the handbooks the students have designed and *Write Source 2000*.

Note: You might extend this discussion by asking your students the following question: What is the difference between *Write Source 2000* and the language arts textbook you used last year? (If possible, have copies on hand.)

Review "Using the Handbook" page in the handbook. Have students practice using *Write Source 2000* with a Scavenger Hunt activity. Have them complete this activity for the next day. (See the previous page for an explanation of scavenger hunt activities.)

DAY 4 Discuss the completed Scavenger Hunt. (Note the answer key on this page for the prepared activity sheets.)

Then have students find one page, one short section, one set of guidelines, one illustration, etc. that they find interesting or entertaining. Students should prepare to share their discoveries on the next day.

DAY 5 Students should present their "finds" in discussion groups or as a class. With any time remaining, select one of the Scavenger Hunt activities (preferably "Easy Liftoff") and see who can get the most correct answers in a specified amount of time.

Answer Key
Scavenger Hunt A

1. 13° N, 122° E
2. flock or gaggle
3. time
4. Students can choose from *buzz, gunk, gushy, swish, zigzag, zing*, or *zip*.
5. Reword the test question into a topic sentence.
6. Be realistic about the goals you set for yourself.
7. a page at the end of a report which lists in alphabetical order the books and materials you have used in your report
8. Reserve a section of a notebook for each class you would like to write about in your log.
9. list of all the latest magazine articles
10. independent clauses which are not connected with a coordinate conjunction (or) independent clauses when the clauses are connected only by a conjunctive adverb
11. inside
12. 2,204.6 pounds

Scavenger Hunt B

1. selecting, collecting, connecting, and correcting
2. Take inventory of people you know or have heard about.
3. The heading includes the sender's complete address and the full date.
4. recalling information
5. together or with
6. a word used in place of a noun
7. Poetry is "imaginary gardens with real toads in them."
8. either, or; neither, nor; not only, but also; both, and; whether, or (See 792 for more)
9. these words are used as names
10. you can divide a word at the end of a line

Easy Liftoff

1. 458
2. personal writing (129-149)
3. 366
4. 14
5. 176
6. hypn
7. right of trial by jury
8. had been found
9. Cracow
10. 350-355

GETTING STARTED SCENARIO
What Would You Put in a Handbook?

■ The scenario you are about to read challenges you to solve a problem—what would you put in a student handbook?

You Have Been Called!

You have been called to New York by Mrs. McGuffey, a famous and successful editor of an equally famous and respected educational publishing company. When you are escorted into her office she surprises you by asking, "What would you put in a student handbook if you wanted students, like you, to *really use* it? I want to publish a handbook so powerful that students will take it to all their classes and then take it home to help them with their homework. That's why I've asked you to come to New York. Will you help us design this handbook?"

What would you put in a student handbook?

What would it look like? What title would you give it?

What would you do to make it easy to use?

Why do you think students would like and use the handbook you have planned?

(Use the space below to start your planning.)

The cover of my book will look like this:

What Would You Put in a Handbook?

■ **When you have completed your plan, review your copy of *Write Source 2000*. Compare the handbook with the one you have designed.**

Compare and Contrast

Is the handbook you designed like ours? Does *Write Source 2000* contain some of the same information you chose to put in the handbook you designed? What different information does your handbook contain?

Same Information	Different Information

Does *Write Source 2000* look like the handbook you designed?

Same Qualities	Different Qualities

Getting to Know the *Write Source 2000* Handbook
SCAVENGER HUNT A

| **If you have not already learned how to use the handbook, read "Using the Handbook" at the front of *Write Source 2000*. Once you understand how your handbook works, use it to answer the questions that follow.**

1. Using the maps in your *Write Source 2000*, identify the lines of **latitude** and **longitude** (in degrees) for the Philippines. _____ and _____

2. A group of **geese** is called a _____ .

3. The **root** *chron* means _____ .

4. Three examples of **onomatopoeia** are _____ ,
_____ , and _____ .

5. What is the main idea of the **minilesson** in "Planning and Writing the Essay Answer"?
_____
_____

6. Identify the first guideline for **setting a goal**. _____
_____

7. A **bibliography** is_____
_____ .

8. What is the first step you would take if you wanted to start a **learning log**?_____
_____
_____

9. The *Readers' Guide* is an organized _____ .

10. A **semicolon** is used to join two _____
_____ .

11. Periods and commas are placed _____ **quotation marks**.

12. How many pounds in one **metric** ton?_____

Getting to Know the *Write Source 2000* Handbook
SCAVENGER HUNT B

If you have not already learned how to use the handbook, read "Using the Handbook" at the front of *Write Source 2000*. Once you understand how your handbook works, use it to answer the questions that follow.

1. Identify the four steps in the **writing process**.

   _____

2. Identify the first "selecting" guideline in **"Writing Phase Biographies."** (Refer to "Biography, writing a" in the index.)

   _____

   _____

3. List the information found in a heading for a **business letter**.

   _____

4. Identify the most basic **level of thinking** you practice in school.

   _____

5. The **prefix** "co" means _____ .

6. A **pronoun** is _____

   _____ .

7. What is Marianne Moore's definition of **poetry**? _____

   _____

8. List three pairs of **correlative conjunctions**. _____

   _____

9. **Capitalize** words such as *mother, father, aunt,* and *uncle* when _____

   _____ .

10. The **dictionary** is often used to check on where _____

    _____ .

Getting to Know My Handbook

Find suitable words to complete the chart below. Be sure the words you select begin with the letters in the left-hand column. Use each word only once. *Note:* You won't necessarily find a word that corresponds to each letter for all of the categories.

	Commonly Misspelled Words	Thinking Terms (See 330)	Computer Terms	Prepositions	Commonly Mixed Pairs (See 574)	Countries I Have Never Seen	Topics I Would Like to Write About
W	weird						
R							
I							
T							
E							
S							
O							
U							
R							
C							
E							

Getting to Know
The *Write Source 2000* Handbook

Easy Liftoff

■ **Do these simple warm-ups and you'll be flying through *Write Source 2000* in no time.**

1. (*Preposterously easy*) Using the table of contents,
   find the topic number where "The Yellow Pages" begin. _____

2. (*Ridiculously easy*) Using the table of contents again, find out which
   major unit contains sections on writing about personal experiences. _____

3. (*Piece of cake*) Using the index of topics at the back of the
   book, find the topic number where you would learn about SQ3R. _____

4. (*Pretty simple*) Starting in the index, find out
   how many lines are in a Shakespearean sonnet. _____

5. (*No sweat*) Find the topic number for the sample news story. _____

6. (*Easier than you think*) What is the root for the word "hypnosis"? _____

7. (*Not too hard*) What is the topic of Amendment 7 to the Constitution of the United
   States?

   _____

8. (*Could be worse*) What is the past perfect passive form of the verb "find"?

   _____

9. (*OK, this is a challenge,
   but you can do it.*) What
   European city is lo-
   cated at 20° east longitude and 50° north latitude?

   _____

10. (*If you can answer this,
    you're airborne!*) Find
    the topic numbers
    where examples of
    "fuzzy thinking" are
    given.

    _____ - _____

Using *Write Source 2000:*
Long-Range Activities

■ Periodically select pages, guidelines, checklists, or models for your students to read and react to in discussion groups or as a class. Instruct students to take note of information they find new, interesting, and helpful with a small check (✓) and information they have questions about with a small question mark (?). The information that is checked or questioned becomes the focus of their discussion. (Students should make their marks in pencil, so they can erase them later on.)

■ On a regular basis conduct minilessons which give your students practice using *Write Source 2000.* (Sample minilessons follow; additional minilessons can be found on pages 93-110.)

I'm stuck, I'm stuck. ....*Breaking Writer's Block*

■ The only sure cure for writer's block is writing anyway. You've got to get back to the start, where you don't give a hoot, where writing is just a fling. To get there,
  READ topic numbers **004** and **005**, "An Invitation to Writing."
  DO exactly what you're told in **005**, "Preparing for Liftoff." When you're done, you won't be preparing anymore. You'll be off!

Me-Maps ....*Creating a "SourceBank"*

■ To build up ideas to write about, read the paragraph on the "Life Map" (**034**).
  TRY a different kind of "Me-Map" like one of these:
  • A "Cut Map"—my best and worst cuts and scrapes
  • A "Sandwich Map"—my best and worst sandwiches
  • A "Talk Map"—how I learned to talk
  • A "Fall Map"—my best and worst trips, plunges, spills, and collapses
  • A "Dare Map"—the best and worst chances I've taken
  INVENT a "Me-Map" of your own.

In, Under, and Around ....*Using Prepositions*

■ Review the rules for using prepositions in "The Yellow Pages" (**788-790**).
  COMPOSE a poem of at least five lines, on any subject, in which each line begins with a different preposition. (See **236** for a model.) SHARE finished products.

Nearsighted ....*Sentence Combining and Conjunctions*

■ Study the guidelines for conjunctions (**792-795**).
  STUDY the "Guidelines for Sentence Combining" (**103-108**).
  FIND something small within an arm's length of where you are sitting and study it.
  WRITE three short sentences about the thing you've seen.
  USING various kinds of conjunctions, COMBINE the three sentences into one; TRY to do it in three different ways.

Writing Programs

The contemporary writing programs described on the following pages offer teachers an opportunity to use a variety of approaches to meet the individual needs of their students.

An Overview
Contemporary Writing Programs

How Were You Taught to Write?

Did your teachers approach writing as a series of skills that had to be learned sequentially? Did they provide literary models that you were to emulate in your own writing? Or, did they perhaps assign compositions on Mondays with little or no direction and expect flawless, finished copies on Fridays?

Do any of these approaches sound familiar? They should. For years, teachers used these methods to "teach" writing. Consider yourself fortunate if you had teachers who provided you with classrooms conducive to real writing and learning.

How is writing taught today?

If you are up on your contemporary writing research, you know this isn't an appropriate question. Writing isn't really taught. That is, writing isn't a set of facts, forms, or formulas that a teacher imparts, and it certainly isn't worksheet busywork. We now know that it is (or should be) a student-centered activity that is learned through a variety of shared writing experiences.

So where does this put the teacher? Not behind his desk lecturing or correcting yesterday's assignments. It puts him right alongside his students; teachers and students write and learn together.

The writing teacher's most important function is to provide the proper mixture of freedom, encouragement, and guidance so that he and his students can learn by doing. He functions much like the understanding parent or personal mentor.

And if writing is not taught, then how is it learned? There are a number of contemporary approaches that promote writing as a student-centered learning activity. All of these approaches have a number of things in common in addition to being student centered.

■ First of all, writing programs don't require a textbook.

Most textbooks by their very nature are prescriptive. That is, they are designed as much to tie students and teachers to the textbook as they are to help students develop as independent thinkers and writers. In a contemporary writing classroom, the students' own writing serves as the textbook. With the support of the necessary reference mate-

rials—a handbook (like *Write Source 2000*), a current dictionary, and a thesaurus—students and teachers help each other develop and grow as writers.

■ Second, the new writing programs are individualized.

In most contemporary writing classrooms, students work and learn individually and in small groups. Instruction is based on need and given when one or more students need help with a basic skill or rhetorical concept. The form of the instruction is usually a 10- to 15-minute minilesson. (See page 94 in this booklet for information on minilessons.) Full-class activities are kept to a minimum so students have as much opportunity as possible to develop their own writing.

■ They are lively and active.

Modern writing programs promote active learning. On any given day, a student might spend his time in a group-critiquing session or writing or reading on his own or helping a classmate sort out a problem with her work. There's no hiding in the last row of the classroom as the teacher lectures.

■ They are well planned.

Just because contemporary writing programs are student centered doesn't mean that students can simply do as they please. Even the most motivated students will take advantage of too much freedom. Deadlines, support materials, methods of instruction, methods for measuring writing progress, and sensible classroom management procedures all have to be established for a program to be successful. Programs must also be flexible enough to meet the needs and interests of the students (obviously within reason) as the course work progresses.

■ They are integrated.

Finally, contemporary writing programs draw from all of the significant research. A particular program won't, for example, be based solely on the writing process approach or on whole language learning. Instead, it will most likely be a blend or combination of approaches. What follows is a brief description of four of the most significant approaches to writing.

Four Approaches to Writing

The Process Approach

While using the process approach, students learn that writing—real writing—is a process of discovery and exploration rather than an end product or a series of basic skills. As students develop their writing, they make use of all steps in the writing process—prewriting, writing the first draft, revising, proofreading, and publishing. And the writing they develop, for the most part, stems from their own thinking and experiences.

Students use prewriting activities to discover writing ideas they know and care about. They are encouraged to talk about their ideas and create a community of writers within the classroom. They write first drafts freely and quickly, and they revise carefully. After editing and proofreading, students share or publish their work.

Write Source 2000 includes a complete discussion of the writing process. (See 011.) You will note that we refer to prewriting activities as *selecting* and *collecting*, writing and revising as *connecting*, editing and proofreading as *correcting*. Also, note that the guidelines for the specific types of writing are organized according to the steps in the writing process. (See pages 46-47 in this booklet for more on the writing process.)

The Whole Language (Thematic) Approach

When using the whole language approach, the teacher (ideally with student input) chooses a theme which serves as the focal point for an intense and thorough whole language experience—that is, an experience which immerses students in a variety of integrated reading, writing, listening, and speaking activities.

The teacher provides pieces of literature and other prewriting activities as starting points for the thematic study. Writing projects evolve from these activities. The writing process approach and usually some form of the writing workshop approach are incorporated into whole language programs.

The *Write Source 2000 Language Series* includes a number of whole language writing units for grades 6, 7, and 8. (See pages 48-49 in this booklet for more on whole language learning.)

The Personal Experience Approach

The focus of this approach is simple: Students enjoy writing and find it meaningful if it stems from their personal experiences and observations. Students usually keep a journal in a personal experience (experiential) program so they always have a number of potential writing ideas to draw from. As with most contemporary approaches, the writing process and some form of a writing workshop are incorporated into the program.

Free writing (rapid writing, spontaneous writing) plays an integral part in this approach to writing as well. Both journal writing and free writing help students write honestly and sincerely about their personal experiences in assigned writing. And it helps students eventually produce writing that readers will find interesting and entertaining.

Review the table of contents in *Write Source 2000*, and you will note that we generally address personal forms of writing before we address more detached, content-oriented forms of writing. It follows that the more students write from personal experience, the better able they are to address increasingly more complex experiences in more sophisticated forms of writing. This writing eventually becomes more and more public, the kind of writing students are often forced to produce long before they're ready.

See *Student-Centered Language Arts K-12* by James Moffett and Betty Jane Wagner (Boynton/Cook, 1992) for more on this approach.

The Writing Workshop Approach

In a writing workshop, students write or work on writing-related issues every day (reading, researching, critiquing, participating in collaborative writing, etc.). They are expected to keep all of their work in writing folders, and they are expected to produce a predetermined number of finished pieces by the end of the term. They are encouraged to take risks, to experiment with new forms and techniques. Support during each writing project comes from both peer and teacher conferences. Students utilize the steps in the writing process to develop their writing and share their work with their group.

The teacher acts as a guide and facilitator. She creates a classroom environment that is conducive to the workshop approach. Desks and chairs are arranged to make student interaction easy. The classroom is stocked with an ample supply of relevant reading and writing materials. Instruction and advice is given when it is needed on an individual basis, in small groups, or to the entire class. Instruction generally takes the form of a minilesson. The teacher also serves as the final editor before a piece is published.

See pages 51-52 in your booklet for more information about writing workshops. Also refer to *In the Middle* by Nancie Atwell (Heinemann-Boynton/Cook, 1987) for a discussion of a middle school workshop program in action.

The "Process" Approach

1. What is writing?
- Writing is thinking on paper.
- Writing is "chasing thinking and turning it into thought."
- Writing is "the exposed edge of thought."

2. What is the "writing process"?
- The "writing process" is the best way we know of to turn thinking into writing.
- The process is usually broken down into four or five manageable steps, allowing students to concentrate on one step at a time.
- The steps in the process are generally broken down into **prewriting**, **writing**, **revising**, **proofreading**, and **publishing**.

3. Why do students write?
(Traditional Objectives)
- To demonstrate the retention of information.
- To improve language skills, especially surface skills (punctuation, spelling, handwriting, . . .).
- To please the teacher.

(Using the Writing Process)
- To explore and to understand their world.
- To learn, discover, to clarify thinking.
- To pass along information.

4. How is writing encouraged?
(Traditional Teacher-Centered Approach)
- Assign a topic, length, time limit.
- Assign an outline and/or "thesis statement."
- Assign an introduction; check for compliance.
- Expect students to produce a "correct" paper.
- Mark, grade, comment.
- Return papers, marked for all errors.
- Request that some students rewrite their assignments until they get it right.

(Student-Centered Approach)
- Students use prewriting activities to discover a topic they know and care about. (See 033-038 in *Write Source 2000* for examples.)
- Students are encouraged to "talk" about their topics to help them develop a sense of purpose for writing.
- Students write for real audiences—usually their peers—rather than for their teachers.

- When students write a first draft, they focus on getting ideas down on paper.
- They think as they go, crossing out, switching directions, using abbreviations, writing rapidly.
- Students revise their writing by going back over what they have written—adding, cutting, replacing, and moving information.
- They read aloud what they have written and discuss it with their peers and/or teacher.
- At this stage, the focus is on ideas, order, clarity, word choice, ways to make the piece more exciting. (See 021 in *Write Source 2000* for more.)
- Students proofread their work only after they have their ideas straight.
- Students work on mechanical problems in small groups, in individual conferences, with the whole class, or by using a handbook of mechanics and usage.
- Students keep their papers until they are ready to share them; then they put their writing in finished form.
- Students publish their work—which might simply mean that their writing is displayed for peers to read.
- The teacher, with student input, grades the finished product.

5. What are the results of using the writing process?

- Students find writing more meaningful because it is a reflection of their own thinking.
- Students develop a feel for real writing.
- Students develop independent thinking skills and take pride in their work.
- Students develop a better attitude toward writing which results in better writing from students of all abilities.
- Using the writing process means less work for teachers.

6. How often should students be given an opportunity to use the writing process?

- At least twice a week (minimum of 20 minutes each).
- Ideally, four or five times a week (allowing enough time for students to finish their work).

7. What do current guides to curriculum planning say about writing and the writing process?

(We happen to be located in Wisconsin. Our DPI produces an excellent guide to curriculum planning from which the following information was taken.)

The Language Arts Task Force recommends the following about writing:

- Curriculum and instruction in writing reflect the knowledge that we learn language holistically, through whole problems in creating meaning, rather than through practice in isolated skills.
- Texts reinforce and support the teaching that has already gone on within the writing process.
- Writing should be a schoolwide activity, integrated into content-area learning at all levels.
- Students at all levels do original writing every week, gaining consistent experience in working through the entire writing process.
- Teachers view writing as a developmental process rather than an accumulation of skills.
- Curriculum and instruction recognize the contribution of current research and effective classroom practice.
- Each district should develop a consistent K-12 philosophy for the teaching of writing.

The Task Force also recognizes the following:

- Formal grammar study improves neither student writing nor standard usage.
- "Grammar" should be taught in the context of actual oral and written communication.
- Sentence diagramming, labeling parts of speech, and having students memorize lists of rules are traditional practices which should be avoided.
- Sentence combining, sentence expansion, and sentence transformation are worthwhile classroom practices.
- Students must be taught how to revise, then given regular opportunities to practice.
- Daily oral language activities can be very worthwhile.

8. Why is it important for all teachers to know about the writing process?

- When implemented properly, it can change the effectiveness of the entire school system—in all areas.
- A districtwide implementation of the writing process would provide continuity within the K-12 writing program.
- Using the writing process in all its forms significantly enhances learning in all subjects.
- The writing process works well with all forms of learning, especially thinking and cooperative learning.
- A curriculum based on the writing process sets its own goals and priorities rather than yielding to those set by publishers of textbooks and standardized tests.

9. What else does a teacher need to know before using the writing process?

- Students need a lot of practice using the writing process to get a real feel for it.
- *Write Source 2000* provides a chapter on the writing process (011) that should be read and discussed with your students at the beginning of the year.
- Also review with your students "Starting Points" (030)—a handy writing-process resource students will refer to time and time again as they develop their writing.
- Point out that all the guidelines for writing assignments in *Write Source 2000* are arranged according to the writing process.

The Whole Language Approach . . .

Whole language isn't just for language arts teachers. Teachers of music, social studies, art, math, or any other subject can also be whole language teachers. By integrating reading, writing, speaking, and listening activities into specific content areas, teachers can provide students with whole language experiences, ones that will actively involve them in learning.

A whole language program supports learning across the curriculum. Here's how teachers can apply whole language the whole day:

Incorporate reading . . .

- Provide plenty of reading material relevant to your subject area. (Magazines, journals, and biographies are great resources.)
- Within certain limits, allow students to choose their own reading material.
- Allow time for SSR (sustained silent reading).
- Provide students time to react to and share their reading.
- Encourage the reading of a wide variety of research materials that are authentic and meaningful; also encourage personal interviews, site visits, and discussions with friends and relatives (from which subsequent recommendations and motivation for reading may come). (See 360-387 in *Write Source 2000* for more information.)

Incorporate listening . . .

- Make listening an important part of the daily activities.
- Practice listening techniques and help students develop skills for effective listening.
- Build listening skills within the context of daily activities; avoid using too many isolated drills and exercises.
- Encourage students to interview people they (the students) are interested in.
- Arrange for speakers who are willing to tell their stories and share their experiences.
- Help students identify each speaker's purpose and their own purpose for listening. (See 402 in the handbook for more information and the *Write Source 2000 Language Series* for student activities.)

Incorporate writing . . .

- Allow students the freedom to choose what they want to write.
- Provide students with examples of interesting writing.
- Promote writing as a process (rather than a set of skills or an end product).
- Let students write for different audiences: classmates, contest judges, newspaper and magazine editors, friends and relatives.
- Use writing-to-learn activities: journal writing, learning logs, stop 'n' write, exit slips, admit slips, etc. Writing-to-learn activities are ungraded and free from traditional teacher evaluation. (See 409-412 in the handbook for more information.)

Incorporate speaking . . .

- Provide students with a wide range of speaking opportunities relevant to their interests and experiences.
- Stimulate discussion by asking questions and providing feedback.
- Give students at all levels frequent opportunities to create classroom dramas.
- Make use of video and audio equipment, filmstrips, overhead projectors, computers, and other technological equipment. (See 388-407 in the handbook for more information on incorporating speaking into classroom activities.)

Listening, speaking, reading, and writing are not "subjects" like biology or geography. Children don't read reading or write writing or speak speech. Rather, they employ the language arts in all their learning. In that way, the language arts are central to the entire curriculum and should be actively planned for and taught in all areas, grades K-12.
—**A Guide to Curriculum Planning in English Language Arts,** *Wis. Dept. of Public Instruction*

An Approach for All Teachers

Here's how whole language teachers approach learning in their classrooms:

- You'll find teachers and students working together as active participants in the learning process.

- Writing, reading, speaking, and listening are everyday tools for learning.

- Teachers see reading, writing, speaking, and listening as complementary strands of language learning, and incorporate them throughout the day.

- The students' personal classroom experiences are open-ended, shaped by their input.

- Teachers provide opportunities for students to connect with real-life events.

- There is shared decision making. Everyone participates in the decision-making process, including decisions about materials, activities, and evaluation.

> *"The secret of education is respecting the pupil."*
> —Ralph Waldo Emerson

- Students have opportunities for cooperative learning and peer conferencing (sharing and tutoring).

- There is respect for the ideas and interests of others. It is understood that each learner has something valuable and important to contribute.

- Instruction is student directed; students influence what is talked about and being taught.

- Every child works at his or her ability level and therefore experiences success.

- Activities are considered "invitations" rather than assignments. Students are invited to read, write, and explore topics that are of interest to them.

- Reading, writing, speaking, and listening are integrated to create theme studies across the content areas.

- Errors are considered a source of information rather than a sign of failure. Risk taking produces errors, and students learn by those errors.

- Evaluation is ongoing. Evaluations are made primarily on a personal basis, and each student is seen as unique. Self-evaluation is an important part of the whole language process.

- Teachers observe students and continually evaluate and improve their programs based on those observations.

- For more characteristics of a whole language classroom refer to the following titles:

  What's Whole in Whole Language – Ken Goodman

  Whole Language: Theory in Use – Judith Newman

  The Whole Language Evaluation Book – Edited by Ken and Yetta Goodman and Wendy Hood

> *"A school should not be a preparation for life. A school should be life."*
> —Elbert Hubbard

In a whole language classroom students are encouraged to make learning connections "outside" of school.

The Personal Experience Approach

"I can tap into [my students] human instincts to write if I help them realize that their lives and memories are worth telling stories about, and if I help them zoom in on topics of fundamental importance to them."
—writing teacher June Gould

We know from firsthand experience that the personal stories young learners love to share can serve as the basis of an effective and lively writing program. Here's how we did it:

Getting Started

At the beginning of the school year, we introduced in-class journal writing to the students. (We encouraged students to write outside of class in journals as well, but the journals in school were part of our writing program.) We knew that the most effective way to get students into writing was simply to let them write often and freely about their own lives, without having to worry about grades or turning their writing in. This helped them develop a feel for writing, real writing, writing that originates from their own thoughts and feelings.

That's where the journals come in. No other activity that we know of gets students into writing more effectively than personal journal writing. (And no other type of writing is so easy to implement.) All your students need are spiral notebooks, pens, time to write, and encouragement to explore whatever is on their minds. (See 130 in the handbook for more information.)

 **Helpful HINT**

We provided our students with four or five personal writing prompts each time they wrote. They could use one of these prompts as a starting point for their writing if they wished. The choice was theirs. (We found that providing writing prompts was much easier and more productive than going into our "You've got plenty to write about" song and dance.)

Writing Prompts

Here's a typical list of one day's writing prompts: Write about

- your most memorable kitchen-related experience,
- coping with younger brothers or sisters,
- being home alone, late at night,

- or what you did over the past weekend.

(See 039 in the handbook for a list of writing prompts.)

We would ask our students to write every other day for the first 10 minutes of the class period. Students knew that every Monday, Wednesday, and Friday were writing days. Of course, we had to adjust our schedule at times, but, for the most part, we tried to stick to writing every other day.

Keeping It Going

After everyone was seated and roll was taken, the journals were passed out, the prompts were given, and everyone wrote. We expected students to write for the complete 10 minutes nonstop. And we made sure that they did. They knew that they would be given a quarter journal grade for the number of words they produced. This almost made a contest out of the writing sessions. Each time they wrote, they wanted to see if they could increase their production from past journal entries, and they always wanted to write more than their classmates.

"Over the last fifteen years, a number of teachers around the country and their students have been amazed by what happened when people write ten to fifteen minutes without worrying about grammar, punctuation, or spelling, and concentrating only on telling some kind of truth."
—Ken Macrorie

Wrapping It Up

On days that we weren't writing, we shared journal entries. First, students would exchange journals with a classmate. They would count the number of words in the entry, read it carefully, and then make comments on things they liked or questioned. After they shared their comments among themselves, we would talk about the entries as a class.

The writers themselves would be reluctant to share their entries with the entire class. But the readers had no problem volunteering someone else's entry ("You've got to hear Nick's story") and reading it out loud. The students loved these readings and the discussions which followed.

Personal Experience Papers

Periodically, we would interrupt the normal course of journal writing and sharing and make formal writing assignments. That is, we would ask students to review their entries and select one (or part of one) to develop into a more polished, complete personal experience paper. Usually, those entries that readers enjoyed and wanted to know more about would be the ones the young writers would choose to develop.

We wanted to make sure that their writing went through at least one or two thorough revisions, so we gave our writers plenty of class time to work on their papers. They also were required to turn in all of their preliminary work with their final drafts. (See "Writing About Experiences," 144, in the handbook for guidelines for this type of writing.)

The experience papers were shared with the entire class at the end of the project. This was a fun and informal activity, but one that students came to appreciate as an important part of the entire composing process. It was their day. They were on stage. They were sharing the end product of all of their work—a special moment in their own lives.

Events for the First Week
The Writing Workshop Approach

See a writing workshop in action by studying the sample schedule on the following page. Here you will find how one teacher organized his writing workshop. This schedule reserves time for minilessons, status checks, individual or group work, and sharing sessions. Adjust this schedule accordingly.

Since this schedule is designed for one of the first weeks of a workshop, all students are asked to participate in the minilessons. In time, you can meet the needs of your students by inviting only those attempting certain goals to do minilessons. All other students will be actively engaged with a piece of writing or another option you have offered.

Note: For additional information on the writing workshop approach, please see page 45 in this booklet. Also, refer to Nancie Atwell's *In the Middle* (see page 92) for invaluable suggestions for setting up a writing workshop.

Instructor Checklist—
A Management Tool

One management technique that teachers of workshops advocate is the use of a checklist similar to the one shown on the right. The teacher designs the checklist after he or she has set up a weekly schedule. Such a checklist serves as a quick reference for you as the week unfolds, and as a history as the year proceeds. It is also valuable if you want to show other teachers, administrators, or parents what your students are doing in their writing workshop.

❑ **Cover minilessons.**

   ❑ **011, 012, 013** (Introduction to writing process and choosing a subject)

   ❑ **033-034** (Creating a "SourceBank")

   ❑ **035-036** (Activities to help discover and select a subject)

   ❑ **130-132** (Journal keeping)

   ❑ **014-019** (Collecting and writing an opening or lead)

   ❑ **037-038** (Searching and shaping activities)

   ❑ **020** (Writing the first draft)

❑ **Teach two reading-to-learn strategies.**

   ❑ Tell/retell

   ❑ Smart

❑ **All students receive writing folders.**

❑ **Students experiment with free writing and clustering.**

❑ **Students make three journal entries.**

❑ **Students experiment with additional starting techniques.**

❑ **Students write a lead paragraph.**

❑ **Students work on a first draft.**

❑ **Students write exit slips.**

* See the **weekly schedule** for a writing workshop on the following page.

Writing Workshop: Weekly Schedule

This schedule can vary depending on the teacher's needs. A teacher might, for example, conduct writing workshops for three days a week and reading workshops for the other two days. (See page 68 in your booklet for a schedule for the first week in a reading workshop.)

MONDAY	TUESDAY	WEDNESDAY	THURSDAY	FRIDAY
Writing Minilesson #5 10 MIN.	**Writing Minilesson #6** 10 MIN.	**Writing Minilesson #7** 10 MIN.	**Writing Minilesson #8** 10 MIN.	**Quiz or Review of Minilessons #5 - #8** 10 MIN.
Status Check 2 MIN. (Find out what students will work on for the day.	**Status Check** 2 MIN.	**Status Check** 2 MIN.	**Status Check** 2 MIN.	**Status Check** 2 MIN.
Individual Work Writing, Revising, Editing, Conferencing, or Publishing 30 MIN.	**Individual Work** Writing, Revising, Editing, Conferencing, or Publishing 30 MIN.	**Individual Work** Writing, Revising, Editing, Conferencing, or Publishing 30 MIN.	**Individual Work** Writing, Revising, Editing, Conferencing, or Publishing 30 MIN.	**Individual Work** Writing, Revising, Editing, Conferencing, or Publishing 30 MIN.
Whole Class Sharing Session 5 MIN.	**Whole Class Sharing Session** 5 MIN.	**Whole Class Sharing Session** 5 MIN.	**Whole Class Sharing Session** 5 MIN.	**Whole Class Sharing Session** 5 MIN.

Classroom Strategies

The classroom strategies which follow cover a number of areas often overlooked in contemporary writing programs.

An Overview
Evaluating Student Writing

Two kinds of evaluation interest teachers today. **Formative** (evaluating while the student is "forming" the project) and **summative** (evaluating the total outcome, or sum, of the student's effort). Formative evaluation does not result in a grade; summative evaluation does. Some teachers do choose, however, to give students a set number of points during different stages in the formative steps in the writing process.

Formative Evaluation

Formative evaluation is most often used for writing-to-learn activities, prewriting activities, writing in progress, journal entries, and so forth. Four types of formative evaluation are widely used:

- Desk-side conference
- Scheduled teacher/student conference
- Written questions and responses
- Peer responses

Note: Make sure your students understand writing as a process. Review "The Writing Process" in the *Write Source 2000* handbook when and if necessary.

DESK-SIDE CONFERENCES occur when a teacher stops at a student's desk to ask questions and make responses while students are working. In the early stages of the writing process, responses and questions should be about writing ideas, content, audience, purpose, generating ideas, and getting those ideas on paper. Questions should be open-ended. This gives the writer "space" to talk. When a writer is talking, he is thinking, clarifying, and making decisions. Teachers should not attempt to solve problems for the students, but instead ask questions and suggest possible solutions.

Respond to a student's paper as a reader, not a teacher. Address "under development," the most common problem young writers face in the first stages of the writing process. Also see the PQS conference format discussed in the next column.

> *"If any man wishes to write in a clear style, let him first be clear in his thoughts."*
> —**Johann Wolfgang von Goethe**

SCHEDULED TEACHER/STUDENT CONFERENCES provide opportunities for students to initiate conferences with you. Student/teacher conferences usually take one of three forms:

- ❑ Student-directed conference
- ❑ PQS conference
- ❑ Small group conference

A student-directed conference may occur when a student has finished a rough draft or a final draft, has identified a problem or need, wishes to establish new criteria for his/her next project, or wishes to share a breakthrough, a success, a "good thing."

A PQS conference (praise-P, question-Q, and suggest-S) will help you refrain from dominating the conference or overteaching. A typical conference lasts from 3 to 5 minutes. First, offer specific and honest praise. Second, ask an appropriate question (one that relates to the writing stage the student is in and one that prompts student talking). Last, offer one or two suggestions. Conferencing becomes easier the more you practice it.

Small group conferences may be groups of three to five students who are at the same stage of the writing process or are experiencing the same problem. The goal of a small group conference is two-fold: first, to help students improve their writing and second, to help students develop as evaluators of writing.

Build a portfolio of student revising samples. Include before and after passages. "Label" these samples and put them in a binder so students can refer to it whenever they need help with their writing.

WRITTEN QUESTIONS AND RESPONSES

help a teacher vary her evaluating techniques, supplement desk-side conferencing, and provide a lasting record.

Collect works in progress. Write comments similar to those you use in conferences and ask open-ended questions so students can actively seek solutions.

In the editing and proofreading stage you can ask, "Why do you need a comma here?" Students must answer the questions and correct the error. However, with inexperienced writers it is best not to mark all of the errors. Draw a double line to indicate where you stopped marking errors.

Students learn just as much from what they are doing right as they do from what they are doing wrong. Make positive comments! Identify good things!

PEER RESPONSES Students can become expert responders, but you must train them. You have already begun to do this in both desk-side and scheduled conferences.

Provide some guide sheets or forms for students to use in peer conferences. (See 029 in *Write Source 2000* for an example guide sheet.) It is best if students work in pairs and have a very limited agenda. Always model how to use the form for your entire class. Impose a time limit to keep students on task (15-20 minutes).

One very simple process to use for peer advising is to ask a student to read his partner's paper and then generate three questions beginning with *who, what, where, when, why,* or *how.* The questions and paper are returned to the writer who responds to these questions. These questions serve as a starting point for a discussion. You can use more elaborate processes as students become better peer responders. (See pages 57-58 in this booklet for ideas. Also see "Group Advising" in *Write Source 2000* for more information.)

> *"At first, I thought, 'Why bother?' What did we know about writing? I resented the group discussions about my writing and offered very few suggestions. Later I realized that we were talking about what we each need right now, for this paper. That was something even a teacher couldn't tell me."*
> —**Paul, a student**

Summative Evaluation

Summative evaluation produces a grade and is used for final papers and projects. Once you assign a grade, the student interprets this as a signal that this piece of writing is finished. We want our students to value the learning process as much if not more than the final product, and we want their attention on personal goals, not grades.

However, the day will come when we must assign a grade. Here are some general principles to help you do that:

1. Clearly establish the criteria for each piece of writing or for each student. Limit the criteria so you do not overwhelm the student or yourself. Establishing criteria for each student during a personal conference will allow you to fit the criteria to the student and his/her learning task.

2. Ask students to help you develop the criteria. This can be done in personal conferences or with the whole class. Students readily accept and understand criteria they have helped build.

3. Students must have ample opportunities for formative evaluation before their final product receives a grade. Students deserve points for the work they have done during the writing process.

4. Concern for content, fluency, and fresh ideas should be of primary concern during summative evaluation for young writers. Mechanical correctness will follow fluency. As students gain control of their language, their errors decrease.

5. Students should be involved in the summative evaluation. A form which asks them to circle the best parts of their writing, list the problems they encountered, draw a squiggly line around parts they would work on if they had more time, and offers space to list the suggestions they tried gives students input. In addition to the above information, they should be asked how much time they put into a project and what grade they would give themselves.

6. You will be very familiar with the piece of writing because of the formative evaluations. You may choose one of the systems listed on the next page to establish a grade.

Suggested Readings for Evaluating Writing:

Inside Out – Kirby and Liner
Learning to Write / Writing to Learn – John S. Mayher, Nancy Lester, Gordon M. Pradl

Approaches for Evaluating Writing

Analytic Scales establish the features necessary for a successful piece of writing and attribute point values for each feature. The grade derives from the point total. Many students like this form of evaluation because it is concrete, and it highlights specific strengths and weaknesses in their writing. The emphasis of analytic scales tends, however, to be on the parts rather than the whole.

Holistic Grading evaluates a piece of writing as a whole. The most basic approach to holistic grading is to read the paper rather quickly for a general impression. The paper is graded according to this impression. A reader might also compare a particular piece with a number of pieces already graded, or grade it for the appearance of elements important to that type of writing. Holistic grading helps teachers reward creativity, inventiveness, and overall effect.

Task-Specific Scoring accords a grade based on how well a student has accomplished specific rhetorical tasks. A teacher might, for example, create a scoring checklist or guide for a short fiction writing assignment. This checklist would include those elements that are inherent in this writing form—plot, characterization, point of view, etc. Students must understand the criteria for scoring before they begin their writing. This type of grading addresses specific rather than open-ended writing assignments.

Portfolio Grading gives students an opportunity to choose pieces of writing to be graded. This is a common method of evaluation in writing workshops. Workshop students compile all of their work in a portfolio or folder. Teachers require them to submit a specified number of finished projects for grading each quarter or semester. Students enjoy this method of evaluation because it gives them some control over the evaluation process; teachers like it because it lessens their work load since they don't have to grade everything a student has written.

A Performance System, as described in *Inside Out*, is a quick and simple method of evaluation. If students complete a writing activity and it meets the previously established level of acceptability, they receive the pre-established grade or points for completing the assignment. The student either has completed the activity or he hasn't. This method works well for evaluating journals.

Responding to Student Writing

The following guidelines will help you assess nongraded and graded writing. (*Writing-to-learn activities, prewriting activities, rough drafts*, and *personal writing* are examples of nongraded writing.)

Responding to Nongraded Writing (Formative)

- Discard your red pens and pencils. Use a #2 pencil when responding to student writing.
- Clarify criteria. Have a clear idea of what you are seeking; make criteria known in advance.
- Scan the writing once quickly. Ask the question, "Has the student understood and responded appropriately to the activity?"
- Reread the writing and indicate that it has or has not fulfilled the requirements of the activity. You may choose to place a check mark on the front page, write a summary sentence on the last page, or note areas needing further attention. (Or you may choose to do all three.)
- React noncritically with positive, supportive language.
- Use marginal dialogue. Resist writing on or over the student's writing.
- Underline points you wish to highlight, question, or confirm. Never circle, cross out, or otherwise undermine the student's writing.
- Respond whenever possible in the form of questions. Nurture curiosity through your inquiries.
- Encourage risk taking.
- Build the product slowly; add criteria carefully.

Evaluating Graded Writing (Summative)

- Ask students to submit prewriting and rough drafts with their final drafts.
- Scan final drafts once, focusing on the writing as a whole.
- Reread them, this time evaluating them for their adherence to previously established criteria.
- Make marginal notations as you read the drafts a second time. Be sure the notations address the process as you evaluate the product. Use supportive language as much as possible.
- Scan the writing a third and final time. Note the feedback you have given. Write a summary comment on the last page of the student's writing, reviewing the positive aspects of the writing, noting progression of ideas, organization, coherency, clarity. Focus on no more than one or two areas which need improvement. End with a positive word of encouragement.
- Assign a grade. The grade should be consistent with the criteria previously established. Remember that you are evaluating both process and product.

Peer Evaluation

Young writers learn to write by writing. No one questions that. But their ability to improve as writers increases significantly if they read a lot. Any professional writer would tell your students it is essential that they become avid readers if they seriously want to learn the craft of writing.

They would also tell your students that it is important to become part of a community of writers. Writers need to talk about writing with other writers. They also need to know that someone just like them—a writer writing—is available when they need help. That's why it's important that your student writers share their work throughout the process of writing. They need to feel that they are among writing colleagues—all committed to helping each other improve as writers.

Note: The reason some teachers find the workshop approach to writing so effective is that it naturally creates a feeling of comradeship among the writers in the classroom.

The exchange of ideas among fellow writers is especially important once they have produced a first or second draft of their work. Writers generally get so close to their writing, so to speak, that they can't always evaluate it objectively themselves. They need their fellow writers, their peers, to ask questions, make suggestions, and offer encouragement. (Use the following minilesson as a possible starting point for peer editing.)

Peer Editing Minilesson

Give each student three pieces of student writing. Erase all names and number papers. Tell  students: "One of these samples is a very good example of student writing. A second is average. A third is poor. Read each paper. Predict which is the best, next best, and weakest. Look at content first. Then look at mechanics."

Ask students for their predictions and then ask them to talk about the strengths and weaknesses they found in each piece of writing. Then tell the students how you would rate these papers and your reasons for doing so.

Types of Evaluating

There generally are three types of evaluation that can go on in a peer conference. There can be a **peer content conference** where student writers share ideas about a piece of writing in progress. The guidelines in "Commenting on Writing" (029) in *Write Source 2000* can be used for these conferences. There can be a **peer editing conference** where student writers help each other with editing a revised draft. See the guidelines listed below for editing conferences. Also refer your students to "Correcting: Preparing the Final Copy" (026) in the handbook. And then there are **peer reaction conferences** where fellow writers actually rate the edited writing. See the general reaction sheet printed on the next page for an example. (Adjust accordingly.)

 Peer evaluation does not replace teacher evaluation (although it could). Obviously, you will want to help your students as much as you can as they develop their writing. And you will want to rate their final products along with at least one peer evaluator.

Editing Conference Guidelines

In an **editing conference** you should:

1. Sit next to the author so that both of you can see the piece of writing.
2. Read the piece of writing back to the author *exactly* as it is written (mistakes and all).
3. Allow the author to stop your reading at any time in order to edit his piece.
4. When the reading is finished and the author has completed his/her corrections, use a highlighting pen to point out other problem words, grammatical errors, or punctuation problems.
5. Sign your name in the upper left-hand corner of the author's first page so that the teacher will know that you helped edit the piece.

Peer Evaluation: Rating Criteria and Sample Reaction Sheet

General Rating Criteria

4 - Excellent	clear, smooth-reading sentences
	descriptive details
	correct mechanics
	imaginative
	appropriate word choice
	effective paragraphing
	(uses transitions)
	recognizable focus
	good organization
3 = Good	recognizable focus
	good transitions
	few mechanical problems
	clear sentences
	some details and creativity
	well organized

2 = Fair	lack of organization
	partial development of topic
	usually complete sentences
	mechanical errors that
	interfere with reading
	faulty paragraphing
1 = Poor	little or no organization
	underdeveloped topic
	many mechanical errors
	hard to follow
0 = Unacceptable	little or no effort
	nearly impossible to read
	no focus on topic
	blank page

REACTING AND REVISING SHEET

EVALUATE: Use the following checklist to help you review and revise your writing. (Use this same checklist to react to your classmates' work.

_____ **Organization:** Is the writing organized so that readers can clearly follow the main ideas?
Is each paragraph complete and easy to follow?

_____ **Detail:** Are all of the important points supported with specific details?
Do all the details provide important information about the subject?

_____ **Style:** Does the writing include effective opening and closing thoughts?
Does the writing read smoothly and easily from start to finish?

_____ **Mechanics:** Has proper attention been given to neatness and accuracy?
(Consider readability, sentences, spelling, usage, and grammar.)

Additional Comments: (when reacting to a classmate's work)

_____ What do you like best about this writing? (List two things.)

_____ Do you have any suggestions for improvements? (List any of these ideas.)

Using Writing Portfolios

"Portfolios have become each student's story of who they are as readers and writers, rich with the evidence of what they are able to do and how they are able to do it."
—Linda Rief

More and more, language arts teachers are making portfolios an important part of their writing programs. Will portfolios work for you? Will they help you and your students assess their writing? Read on and find out.

What is a writing portfolio?

A writing portfolio is a limited collection of a student's writing for evaluation. A portfolio is different from the traditional writing folder. A writing folder (also known as a working folder) contains all of a student's work; a portfolio contains only a student's best efforts.

Why should I ask students to compile writing portfolios?

Having students compile a portfolio makes the whole process of writing so much more meaningful to them. They will more willingly put forth their best efforts as they work on various writing projects, knowing that they are accountable for producing a certain number of finished pieces for publication. They will more thoughtfully approach writing as an involved and recursive process of drafting, sharing, and rewriting, knowing that this process leads to more effective writing. And they will more responsibly craft finished pieces, knowing that their final evaluation depends on the finished products they include in their portfolios.

Any or all methods of assessment can be employed when portfolios are used, including self-evaluation, peer evaluation, contract writing, traditional grading, and so on. (For more on assessment, refer to pp. 54-58 in the *Teacher's Guide*.)

How many pieces of writing should be included in a portfolio?

Although you and your students will best be able to decide this, we advise that students compile at least three pieces of writing in a portfolio each quarter. (Students could contract for a certain amount of required writing.) All of the drafts should be included for each piece. Students should also be required to include a reflective writing or self-critique sheet that assesses their writing progress.

Special Note: Some teachers allow students to include one or two pieces of writing from other disciplines in their portfolios.

When do portfolios work best?

Students need plenty of class time to work on writing if they are going to produce effective portfolios. If they are used right, portfolios turn beginning writers into practicing writers. And practicing writers need regularly scheduled blocks of time to "practice" their craft, to think, talk, and explore options in their writing over and over again.

Portfolios are tailor-made for language arts classrooms that operate as writing workshops. (See the discussion of writing workshops on pp. 51-52 in the *Teacher's Guide* for more information.)

How can I help my students with their portfolio writing?

Allow students to explore topics of genuine interest to them. Also allow them to write for many different purposes and audiences and in many different forms.

In addition, expect students to evaluate their own writing and the writing of their peers as it develops—and help them to do so. (See "Group Advising" in the handbook for help.) Also, provide them with sound guidance when they need help with a writing problem. And create a stimulating classroom environment that encourages students to immerse themselves in writing.

How do I grade a portfolio?

Base each grade on goals you and your students establish at the beginning of the grading period and on what is achieved as evidenced in the portfolio. Many teachers develop a critique sheet for assessment that is based on the goals established by the class. (It's very important that students know how many pieces they should include in their portfolios, how their work should be arranged in their portfolios, how the portfolios will be assessed, and so on.)

What About Grammar?

We do not look at grammar as a traditional course of study in which rules and isolated sentence analysis and diagramming are emphasized. To our way of thinking, grammar study must be closely related to the "real" language of speakers and writers of the standard dialect.

And, we see grammar as best taught in the context of the students' own work. What follows is a list of classroom practices and approaches which promote meaningful context-based grammar instruction—and then a list of traditional approaches which should be avoided as much as possible.

Promoting Meaningful Grammar Instruction

■ Link grammar work as much as possible to the students' own writing.

■ Make editing and proofreading of the students' writing an important part of classroom work. Students should have ready access to a resource for their proofreading. ("The Yellow Pages" in *Write Source 2000* will answer any questions students might have.) They should also have practice editing and proofreading cooperatively.

■ Discover and investigate. Let students learn about grammar for themselves, logically and deductively. For example, the following scenario lets students discover the relationship between a pronoun and its antecedent.

Step 1: Read this sentence.
  The day will begin with a private breakfast where *they* will meet many of the hospital staff who helped *them* cope with the disaster.

Step 2: Answer each of the following questions (orally or in writing).
1. Who are "they" and "them"?
2. What noun could you substitute for these pronouns?
3. Why this noun?
4. Write a sentence which could come before the example sentence. (Use the noun in your sentence.)
5. _____ (the noun) is an antecedent for the pronouns "they" and "them."
6. Define antecedent.

■ Use 10- to 15-minute minilessons or workshop activities for grammar instruction. No one should have to sit through hour-long grammar activities. (See pages 97-100 in your guide for examples.)

■ Make grammar instruction fun as well as instructive. Have students dramatize the parts of speech. Develop grammar games and contests. (See the following page for two ideas.)

■ Immerse students in all aspects of language learning: reading, writing, speaking, listening, and thinking. Putting language to good use comes from using language, in all of its forms, on a regular basis.

Approaches to Use

Sentence combining – Use the students' own writing as much as possible. The rationale behind combining ideas and the proper punctuation for combining should be stressed.

Sentence expansion and revising – Give students practice adding and changing information in sentences they have already created. Also have them expand and revise each other's writing.

Sentence transforming – Students should practice changing sentences from one form to another (from passive to active, beginning a sentence in a different way, using a different form of a particular word, etc.).

Sentence imitation – Students should have practice imitating writing models. According to James Moffett, this activity is a great teacher of grammar because it exposes young writers to the many possibilities of English grammar beyond the basic forms. (See the *Write Source 2000* handbook for guidelines and models.)

Traditional Approaches to Avoid

Sentence diagramming – Traditional diagrams as well as transformational or tree diagrams do not improve a students' ability to edit and proofread their own language use.

Labeling – Analyzing and labeling parts of the sentence offer little or no carryover to the students' own work.

Memorizing – Memorizing abstract rules and definitions also provides little or no carryover to the students' own writing.

Identifying mistakes – Having students identify mistakes or make choices on worksheets does little more than keep students busy, unless you immediately apply the lesson to their own writing.

Daily Oral Practice (Banish Errors!)

It is possible to teach grammar using new and fun activities. Middle school students like these two methods.

MUG (Mechanics, Usage, Grammar) Shots

Time: 5-10 minutes. Sustained practice is the key to success.

Purpose: 1) To identify skills students are misusing. 2) To maintain skills.

Materials: Use sentences from student writing; ask students to write sentences full of errors and to contribute sentences they are currently having trouble correcting.

Method: Write two incorrect sentences on the board. Choose one of the following plans:

PLAN 1:
Each student copies the sentences and corrects them. Secondly, conduct an oral correcting session.

PLAN 2:
Ask students to volunteer corrections orally.

It is most important that students attempt to explain the reason for each correction they offer. Classmates and the teacher may help them zero in on the exact reason. An atmosphere of discovery, cooperation, and investigation helps students risk making corrections. Use "The Yellow Pages" in the handbook.

Special Note: The *Write Source 2000 Language Series* contains a complete set of MUG Shot sentences for each grade level—6, 7, and 8.

Gramo (a game about the parts of speech)

Time: 10-15 minutes or longer if desired.

Purpose: (1) To teach the parts of speech. (2) To let students discover the complexity (and richness) of our language.

Materials: You will have to make the following: Gramo cards (which resemble bingo cards) and a teacher's master card. *See samples on next page.*

Rules: Just like bingo.

1. Players each have a game card and tabs or markers.
2. The teacher has a master card and something to use for markers (bits of paper will do).

3. The teacher calls out a word ("G bug") and players mark on their cards. ("Bug" can be a noun, verb, or adjective.)
4. On a piece of scratch paper students note which word was called and where they marked their card. For example, G-bug-N or G-bug-V.
5. When a player has filled a row, column, or diagonal with markers, he yells out "Gramo."
6. All players wait for the "Gramo" player to recite his answers. (Anyone who thinks they also have a winning card must say "Gramo" before the answers are read aloud.) There can be several winners in one game.
7. If there is a winner (or winners), everyone then clears their card for a new game to begin.
8. If there is no winner (maybe the student who yelled "Gramo" had an incorrect answer), the other players should not clear their cards and that particular game continues until there is a winner.
9. Cards can be traded after a couple of games.
10. Rules can be extended: Play two cards at one time; play four corners.
11. Allow only two wins on one card; then the card must be traded. This keeps top players from monopolizing the game.
12. If a card has "noun" printed in two squares under the same letter ("noun" might be in two squares under the letter "G"), the player may put a marker on each square. This makes that card more valuable.

Helpful HINT

Giving points keeps students on task and acts as a reward. You or a designated student can place a check after each student's name when he/she offers a correction or wins a round of "Gramo."

G	R	A	M	O
Noun	Noun	Noun	Noun	Noun
Verb	Verb	Verb	Verb	Verb
Adjective	Adjective	Adjective	Adjective	Adjective
Preposition	Preposition	Preposition	Preposition	Preposition
Proper Noun	Proper Noun	Proper Noun	Proper Noun	Proper Noun
Conjunction	Conjunction	Conjunction	Conjunction	Conjunction
Adverb	Adverb	Adverb	Adverb	Adverb
Pronoun	Pronoun	Pronoun	Pronoun	Pronoun

Teacher's Master Card

G	R	A	M	O
ADJ	PREP	ADJ	ADVERB	VERB
VERB	NOUN	ADVERB	PREP	PRONOUN
PRONOUN	ADVERB	Free Space	PROPER NOUN	NOUN
CONJ	PROPER NOUN	CONJ	ADJ	ADVERB
NOUN	ADJ	ADVERB	VERB	PREP

Sample Game Card

G R A M O					
		Free Space		

Reading Strategies

The reading strategies
on the following pages can serve
as a basis for an active,
personalized reading program.

A Teacher's Guide for Young Readers
Active Reading

Luke Skywalker,
saggy-jeaned and flanneled,
burst into the room,
slapped his well-read space book
on a desk top,
and started talking of Chewbacca,
Princess Lea, and Death Star
to anyone who would listen.
He bubbled with the discoveries he had made.

Is Luke a typical young reader? We hope so. But maybe that is wishful thinking on our part. We do know for a fact, however, that if you teach in a middle school or junior high you have had at least a few Luke Skywalkers. You know who we are talking about. The young readers who take their books to heart—who get actively involved in their reading with eyes welling or nostrils flaring.

You can accommodate the Luke Skywalkers, and, better yet, spark even your most reluctant readers by promoting ACTIVE READING in your classroom. ACTIVE READING gets students involved. It encourages young readers to read books that are important to them, and it encourages them to explore their thoughts and feelings about their reading. ACTIVE READING not only makes reading enjoyable and meaningful for your students, it develops within them an appreciation for literature.

Here's how you promote ACTIVE READING

Start by encouraging your students to express their feelings in your classroom. This may not sound like much, but you have a lot of "unteaching" to do. Your students have been trained from their very first school activities to stick to the facts, to look for right answers. So give them class time to write freely and honestly about their lives. Ask them for their first impressions to various lessons or activities; seek their emotional responses whenever possible. The more practice, the better.

What does this have to do with ACTIVE READING? Once students feel comfortable talking and writing about their feelings in general, the more apt they will be to get personally engaged in the books they are reading. And once that happens, reading becomes much more than schoolwork; it

becomes, as reading researcher David Bleich states, "a special opportunity [for students] to engage the emotions and thoughts foremost in their minds." And these opportunities are just what the Luke Skywalkers are looking for, and just what might turn your most reluctant readers on to books.

What else can a teacher do to promote ACTIVE READING?

■ Active readers need access to popular young adult and classic titles.

This means that you will need a classroom paperback library well stocked with the most popular titles for young readers. And your students should have easy access to these books. There is nothing more frustrating to ACTIVE READERS than a delay in getting into a new book, or, worse yet, being stuck with a book that bores them. Young readers should have the same freedom as adult readers—to exchange books whenever they are ready to move on to a new one. (See page 72 for a list of popular titles.)

■ ACTIVE READERS need class time to read.

At least one full class period per week should be devoted to reading. If students are given an opportunity to get lost in good books in school, they will be more willing to read outside of class as well. ACTIVE READING in class helps promote ACTIVE READING outside of class (and that can mean less time spent in front of the television).

■ ACTIVE READERS need time to react to their reading.

Young readers like Luke Skywalker have strong feelings and ideas about their reading that they need to express. They can best do this by keeping a journal while they read. Then, whenever they need to react in some way to their reading, they can explore these feelings in their journals.

You might direct them to write a certain number of entries (at least four or five) for each book. You might also suggest that they write at least one entry after the opening chapter, at least three entries during their reading, and one entry after finishing the book. Middle school students can easily write entries of a half page or longer in their journals if they are reading books of their own choosing.

If some of your students have trouble making anything but cursory remarks about their reading, encourage them to write entries nonstop. Uninterrupted writing (5-10 minutes per entry) naturally produces a free flow of ideas and helps students get the feel for exploring their thoughts and feelings.

Questions for journal writing are listed on the next page and in "Keeping a Reading-Response Journal" in this booklet. Also, see "Journal Writing" in *Write Source 2000* for more writing guidelines.

■ ACTIVE READERS need feedback to their journal ideas.

Young readers will appreciate your reaction to their journal entries, during the reading as well as after the reading. Encourage them to submit their entries at any time. This is especially important if they need something clarified during their reading and writing—something that can't wait until the book is completed. This exchange of ideas enhances ACTIVE READING.

You don't have to write long, detailed reactions to a student's entries. Simply show them with sincere comments that you are interested in their ideas.

When you evaluate a reading journal, consider two things. First, consider a student's commitment. That is, ask yourself if a set of journal entries reflects a sincere effort on the part of the writer. Second, consider a student's basic knowledge of the book. Someone who has not read carefully will be hard pressed to produce meaningful journal entries.

See page 68 for a sequence of reading and writing activities from the first week of our active reading program.

■ ACTIVE READERS need time to share their thoughts and feelings with their classmates.

Time should be set aside whenever possible for class or group discussions. During one discussion, your students might share favorite journal entries with the class or their reading group. During another discussion, they might raise certain questions about their reading. (This is especially effective if you have a group of students who have read the same book.) At another time, students might review their books (without giving away the entire plot).

How will ACTIVE READING help you as a teacher?

ACTIVE READING will give you insights into your students' understanding and appreciation of literature. These insights will help you tailor your literature-related activities to the specific needs of your classes. Maybe a certain class has trouble identifying the themes (statements about life) in the books they have read. Another class may have trouble judging the strengths and weaknesses of certain books, while another wants to know more about science fiction books and writers.

ACTIVE READING also offers you an opportunity to challenge your students with stimulating composition assignments. Your ACTIVE READERS will have identified a number of important ideas in their journal writing and discussions that they will want to develop further. Students are much more willing to develop thoughtful writing assignments when they are based on their own discoveries and ideas.

Special Note: In order for ACTIVE READING to work, you must establish certain guidelines. Students must know that reading time is not free time, but time to read or react to their reading. They must also know that they can't waste reading time by simply picking through your paperback library. Finally, it is important that you serve as a reading role model. Read and react along with your classes (at least at the start of the program) so students realize that you take ACTIVE READING seriously.

(If you feel that you need more direction in implementing an ACTIVE READING program, refer to Nancie Atwell's book *In the Middle* in which she describes her successful reading program in great detail.

Questions for Reading Journals

Use these questions to help your students write in their reading journals. This list is not meant to cover all of the issues that might concern your students as they write, and it should be used only when they need a starting point for a journal entry. Their own thoughts and feelings are always the best source for their writing. (See "Keeping a Reading-Response Journal" in your booklet for a more in-depth list of questions.)

1. What were your feelings after reading the opening chapter(s) of this book? After reading half of the book? After finishing the book?

2. Did this book make you laugh? Cry? Cringe? Smile? Cheer? Explode? Explain your reaction.

3. What connections are there between the book and your own life? Explain.

4. What are the best parts of this book? Why? What are the worst parts of this book? Why?

5. What is the author saying about life and living through this book? Explain.

6. What parts of the book seem most believable? Why? What parts seem unbelievable? Why?

> *"The primary subject matter for the reader is the web of feelings, sensations, images, and ideas that he weaves between himself and the text."*
> —Louise Rosenblatt

7. Do you like the ending of the book? Why or why not? Do you think there is more to tell? What do you think might happen next?

8. What do you feel is the most important word in the book? The most important passage? The most important element (an event, a character, a feeling, a place, a decision)? Why is it important?

9. In what ways are you like any of the characters? Explain.

10. Do any of the characters remind you of friends, family members, or classmates? Explain.

11. What character would you like to be in this book? Why? What personality traits of this character would you like to acquire? Explain.

12. What would you and your favorite character talk about in your first conversation? Begin the conversation.

13. Do you think the title fits the book? Why or why not?

14. What makes you wonder in this book? Why? What confuses you in this book? Why?

15. What came as a surprise in the book? Why?

16. Has this book helped you in any way? Explain.

17. How have you changed after reading this book? Explain.

18. How do you picture the author of this book? Why do you picture him or her in this way?

19. What questions would you like answered after reading this book?

20. Who else should read this book? Why? Who shouldn't read this book? Why?

Active Reading Survey

If you plan on implementing an ACTIVE READING program, you might want your students to complete a reading survey to get a feel for their attitude about reading and their experience (or lack of it) as an ACTIVE READER. (The model survey which follows is an adaptation of the reading survey included in Appendix F of *In the Middle* by Nancie Atwell.)

1. If you had to guess . . .
   How many books do you own?
   How many books are there in your house?
   How many novels have you read in the past year?

2. What kind of books do you like to read?

3. How do you decide what books to read?

4. Have you ever reread a book?
   If so, list those titles you can remember.

5. Do you ever read at home for pleasure?
   If so, how often?

6. Who are your favorite authors?

7. In general, how do you feel about reading?

Active Reading
Keeping a Reading-Response Journal

While students are "experiencing" a book, they should be encouraged to record their journey in a journal. Set aside class time specifically for journal writing. Students can use the following ideas as starting points for their writing, but encourage them to explore whatever issues they feel are important. (See "Active Reading" in this book for information on managing journal writing.)

Plot and Character
- Simply "free write" about the book for 5-10 minutes each day.
- Write a description of the character you think is the main character after reading the first chapter.
- After reading several chapters (or about half the book), predict what you think will happen.
- Write a short summary of every chapter (or every 10-15 pages if the chapters are long).
- When you are about halfway through the book, list the characters and briefly tell how you feel about each one of them. Do this again when you have completed the book. Did your feelings change?
- What character do you feel closest to after the first chapter? After you're halfway through the book? Why? Is this the same character you feel closest to when the book ends?
- Keep a time line or "chronolog" of events as they happen.
- Write a dialogue between you and one of the characters. What would you ask this character? How would he/she respond?
- How does the main character interact with other people? Do you like the way he/she treats other people?

Setting and Theme
- Write a description, draw a picture, or create a map of the setting(s).
- If your book is set in a particular country or place, jot down sentences that give you an idea of what that place is like. If your book occurs at a particular time in history, can you gather information about that time from this book? If so, make a list of your findings. If your book takes place in a small town during World War II, write in your own words what living there at that time must have been like. Did they have radio? Television? Cars? What songs were popular?

- Ask yourself this question: "What is the author trying to tell me in this book?"
- Identify important words or phrases in the book. Explain why they are important.
- Paste into your journal any newspaper or magazine articles you find which relate to the book or its themes in any way. You might want to search for some critiques of this book in the library, make copies, and include them.

Personal Reaction
- Make a list of the many different ways you feel while you read. *Uneasy? Fearful? Crushed? Restless? Worried? Hopeful? Annoyed? Peaceful? Free? Sympathetic?* Your class or some groups might choose to make a list of all the feelings that seem to be experienced when reading books.
- Record what was happening in the book when you were having a particular feeling. ("I was angry when . . . .")
- Pinpoint where you were in the book when you became so involved you didn't want to quit reading.
- What memories is this book triggering in you? List these memories and choose one or more to describe in greater detail.
- What new thoughts or ideas come to you as you are reading this book? Keep a list.
- Record anything that seems really important to you while you are reading.

Style and Word Choice
- Copy those sentences, quotes, and passages that move you in some way.
- Make a list of words from the book that you would like to know and use in your own writing.
- What skill are you working on as a writer? Watch how the author of this book uses that skill. Are you learning to *show* instead of *tell*? Copy some sentences or passages which you feel are excellent examples of this skill. Are you learning to write dialogue? How does this author get into and out of dialogue? Copy a few samples for your use.

Final Note: Discuss with your classmates the different techniques you are using for keeping a response journal. Find out what they are using and what is working well for them. Brainstorm together for other techniques that you might try.

Reading-Response Journal Workshop:

A Sample Sequence of Events for the First Week

Time	MONDAY	TUESDAY	WEDNESDAY	THURSDAY	FRIDAY
8:00-8:15	Explain response journals and provide students with ideas for responses. (See page 67 in this booklet.)	Independent Reading & Responding		Read some exit slips to students. Discuss what groups did well and what can make the next sharing session even better.	**Small Group** Share one or two of your journal responses.
8:15-8:30	Students choose a book.			**Second Minilesson:** Group Skills (See 432-449 in *Write Source 2000*.)*	Optional time for groups who are still active. Other groups begin independently reading.
8:30-8:50	**Silent Reading**	**Minilesson Group Skills** (See 432-449 in *Write Source 2000*.)*	**First Small Group** Tell group members what book you are reading and share one or two of your journal responses.	Independent Reading & Responding	
8:50-8:55	Write a journal response.	Pairs may need this time to complete group skill work. Other students may choose journal responses to share.	**Exit Slip** What did my group do well today?		
					Have a nice weekend!

HOMEWORK: For two or three nights during the week, assign students to read and respond for at least 30 minutes on their own. (Optional.)

*Pair students. One student reads aloud the information about one group skill. The other student listens and retells what he/she has heard. Switch roles for the next group skills session.

Reading to Learn
Real Questions for Real People

Asking students to search their own experiences when they read brings reading to a deeper personal level—a level where they can engage and share. The information and sample questions which follow should help you and your students make reading more personal.

Books are full of real people—people with real needs, problems, gifts, talents, skills, questions, and so on. But, too often, when we discuss books with our students, we don't discuss people; instead, we discuss plot, theme, mood, point of view, style, tone, setting, characterization, or some combination of all of these. In doing so, we may be unknowingly moving our students away from instead of toward reading.

Our intentions in discussing plot, theme, style, etc. are good. We want them to develop a finer understanding and appreciation of books. But middle school students are more apt to become life-long readers if we let them identify with characters, relating their own lives to those of the characters.

By searching the text for "real-life" issues, students will find another avenue to comprehension and appreciation, an opportunity to improve their understanding of the human condition, and a chance to actively pursue "ownership" of their reading.

Two prerequisites for effective use of "real-life" questions follow:

First: A classroom climate has to be established that promotes expression of real thoughts and feelings. Having your students write and share entries in personal journals will help build the right classroom climate for "real-life" questions.

Second: Understand that middle school students are particularly interested in the following areas: friendship, family relationships, peer behavior, coping, relating to individual differences, other cultures, understanding male and female, and adopting personal values.

When your class is ready to tackle "real-life" questions, the following steps will help you successfully initiate this activity.

Step 1: Give students sample questions. Use the ones we include on the following page or compose your own.

Step 2: Select a short story to read together. Ask students to watch for and note "real" questions while they read. You may choose to collect their questions or ask them to present them orally. The method you use will depend on how "safe" your classroom environment has become.

Step 3a: If you collect questions, you can now compose a discussion question(s) using the student responses.

Step 3b: If you ask students to present their questions orally, select one and begin a whole class discussion.

Step 4: The whole class discussion serves as a model for the small group discussions that will become the norm. Using small groups will give all students more opportunities to participate and provide an atmosphere which promotes risk taking. Some students feel that sharing real feelings and thoughts is risky until they've practiced it awhile.

Step 5: The following day students should participate in small groups after reading another short story. The instructor may create a "real" question for these discussions.

Step 6: Ask students to watch for "real" questions as they read. Whenever they find one, they should write it down and put it in a box designed for this purpose. These contributions are not signed.

Step 7: Designated students (or the instructor) can select questions for discussion which are appropriate for the reading they are doing and will help students make meaning out of their lives.

Sample Questions

1. **Was** *(name of character)* **obsessed with how she/he looked?**

   ■ Do some age groups seem to be more obsessed with how they look? What age groups are particularly interested in how they look?

   ■ How do you know when someone is obsessed with how he or she looks?

   ■ How do you feel about someone who is obsessed with his or her appearance? How do you feel if this person is someone your own age? Someone who is 40? Someone of another race or culture?

   ■ Is it easier for a boy who is not handsome to be socially accepted and happy than it is for a girl who is not pretty?

2. **Did** *(name of character)* **use a brother/sister/ someone else as a standard for comparison?**

   ■ Do you often compare yourself with someone?

   ■ Do you personally know the person you use for comparison or is it someone famous?

   ■ Do you compare to make yourself feel better?

   ■ Does your comparison ever make you feel inferior?

   ■ What criteria do you use for comparison?

3. **Did** *(name of character)* **have a boyfriend/girl-friend?**

   ■ Why do you think they liked each other?

   ■ Did they have any problems staying friends?

   ■ Was coping with sexuality a problem for them?

   ■ Is coping with sexuality a major problem for most teenagers today?

   ■ Is coping with sexuality made easier or harder by your peers? By your parents? By other adults? By advertising? How is it easier? How is it harder?

   ■ Do adults ever seem to have problems coping with sexuality?

4. **Did** *(name of character)* **have a close relation-ship with an adult?**

   ■ Was this relationship a positive one?

   ■ How could parents of people your age get close to you in order to help you with difficulties?

   ■ Are you willing to express your thoughts and feelings to adults? To parents? To teachers? Why? Why not?

5. **Did** *(name of character)* **use shocking lan-guage?**

   ■ If yes, why? If no, why not?

   ■ Did _____ use shocking language all the time? If yes, why? If no, why not? When didn't _____ use shocking language? What does this careful choice of language tell you about _____'s insides?

   ■ How did cursing make _____ feel? How do you feel about _____'s choice of words?

   ■ Do you curse? Why? When? Why not?

   ■ Does cursing make you feel more powerful? More "in"? More adult? More _____ ? Less _____ ?

   ■ Are you feeling a bit uneasy about discussing cursing? Why? Why not?

6. **How did** *(name of character)* **feel when he/she perceived that** *(name of character)* **disap-proved of him/her?**

   ■ How did _____ cope with _____'s disapproval? Rejection?

   ■ How do you feel when you perceive someone disapproves of you or something you are do-ing?

When students are asked to give personal opin-ions and personal reactions to the books they read, it is not possible to grade them. How can you evaluate your students in these situations? You might find the following criteria useful:

1. How much classroom time does a student spend on reading and reacting?

2. What is the intensity of his/her concentration?

3. How much enthusiasm does he/she express?

4. What degree of care does the student show?

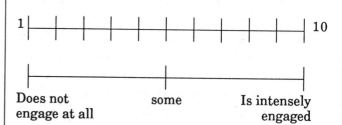

Reading for Pleasure

Experiencing Literature

We must give students an opportunity to read for pleasure. We must let them lose themselves in a book or other pieces of writing without asking for a response or conducting an evaluation.

We must give them time... time to discover all the worlds and feelings and people who live between the covers of books. We must give them time and space to experience reading like Emily Dickinson did... "If I read a book and it makes my whole body so cold that no fire can ever warm me, I know *that* is poetry. If I feel physically as if the top of my head were taken off, I know *that* is poetry. These are the only ways I know it. Is there any other way?"

When we set aside a class period or a portion of a period for pleasure reading, we should model for them the pleasure of reading. This is not a time to correct papers or catch up on paperwork from the front office.

Reading for pleasure means we reduce the rules to the bare minimum. We allow students to abandon a book or read two or three books simultaneously. And, we allow them to share their thoughts and feelings about their reading. (See "Active Reading" in this booklet for more.)

The following four rules should be all that is required for pleasure reading to work in your classroom.

- Have book in hand when it is time for pleasure reading to begin.
- Read for the entire time.
- No homework is to be worked on.
- Do not talk or disturb others.

"There has been a conceptual shift in the way many researchers and teachers think about reading which gives students a much more active role in the learning and reading comprehension process. This shift is reflected in changes from packaged reading programs to experience with books and from concentration on isolated skills to practice reading and writing activities."
—**Reading Report Card NAEP (1985)**

Pleasure Reading in Action

Here are three effective, pleasurable reading activities for you and your students to try.

Many people still love to hear a book read. Once upon a time it was traditional for teachers to read to students for 10 minutes in the morning and after "noon hour," and, believe it or not, they still do. When you read to your students, you are showing them how to give voice to characters, how to let feelings flow, how to interpret a book. When you read aloud to your students, you are giving them something to share and a chance to wonder together. Sharing a book is a pleasurable way for teachers and students to really get to know each other.

It is true you will not be able to evaluate reading for pleasure, but you can be assured that your students are imagining, anticipating, identifying, and empathizing . . . building a zeal for reading.

Brown Bag Reading is also pleasurable. What is it? Give each student a brown bag. They write their name and a subject of keen interest on the outside of the bag. Each student announces his subject to his classmates and then waits to see what will appear in his bag. That is, he waits to see what a classmate or the teacher slips into his bag. It may be merely a quote or a note telling him/her where he can find a magazine article on this subject. It may be a book or an article clipped from a newspaper. It may be a piece of writing by a student who has the same interest and wishes to share some thoughts or a classroom report from another year. Periodically you can have a "reading for pleasure" session where students can discover what is in their "reading bags." Let students change topics when they wish.

Chew! is also pleasurable. What is "Chew!"? It is a very peaceful and pleasurable way to spend a lunch hour. Students arrive with both a lunch to chew and a book to "chew." (The rules for pleasure reading listed in the first column still apply.)

We all know reading is a pleasure. Let's do everything we can to be sure our students discover reading for pleasure... that they discover again or possibly for the first time that reading makes them giggle and shake, wiggle and wonder, sniffle and sigh.

Middle and Junior High School
Popular Titles for a Classroom Library

The titles grouped below are recommended for use in the middle school as classroom library sets. These popular titles can help promote the reading-writing connection by making reading fun and worth writing about. With a little encouragement and direction, students will be eager to explore their thoughts and feelings about these titles in journals and reading notebooks.

GRADE LEVEL 4

Anastasia Krupnik .... Lowry
Best Christmas Pageant Ever .... Robinson
Borrowers .... Norton
Bunnicula .... Howe
Chocolate Fever .... Smith
18th Emergency .... Byars
Fat Men From Space .... Pinkwater
Felicia, the Critic .... Conford
Ferret in the Bedroom,
   Lizards in the Fridge .... Wallace
Fourth Grade Celebrity .... Giff
Frankenstein Moved in on
   the Fourth Floor .... Levy
Henry and Ribsy .... Cleary
Hot and Cold Summer .... Hurwitz
In the Year of the Boar .... Lord
Just Tell Me When We're Dead! .... Clifford
Misty of Chincoteague .... Henry
Owls in the Family .... Mowat
Ralph S. Mouse .... Cleary
Soup for President .... Peck
Strawberry Girl .... Lenski
Stuart Little .... White
Summer of the Monkeys .... Rawls
Superfudge .... Blume
Tales of a 4th Grade Nothing .... Blume

GRADE LEVEL 7

All Creatures Great & Small .... Herriot
Are You in the House Alone? .... Peck
Banner in the Sky .... Ullman
Can You Sue Your Parents
   for Malpractice? .... Danziger
The Cat Ate My Gymsuit .... Danziger
Dawn: Portrait of a Teenage Runaway ..... Sorel
The Day They Came to
   Arrest the Book .... Hentoff
Deenie .... Blume
Durango Street .... Bonham
Fifteen .... Cleary
Fingers .... Sleator
Friends 'til the End .... Strasser
Hold Fast .... Major
Interstellar Pig .... Sleator
It's Not the End of the World .... Blume
Jean and Johnny .... Cleary
The Luckiest Girl .... Cleary
No Promises in the Wind .... Hunt
Pardon Me, You're Stepping on
   My Eyeball .... Zindel
Rifles for Watie .... Keith
Swiftly Tilting Planet .... L'Engle
Tex .... Hinton
There's a Bat in Bunk Five .... Danziger
The Undertaker's Gone Bananas .... Zindel

GRADE LEVEL 5

Anastasia Has the Answers .... Lowry
Are You There, God? It's Me,
   Margaret .... Blume
Beetles, Lightly Toasted .... Naylor
BFG .... Dahl
Black Pearl .... O'Dell
Borrowers .... Norton
The Cat Ate My Gymsuit .... Danziger
Dicey's Song .... Voigt
Harriet the Spy .... Fitzhugh
Hatchet .... Paulsen
Homesick, My Own Story .... Fritz
Indian in the Cupboard .... Banks
Island of the Blue Dolphins .... O'Dell
James and the Giant Peach .... Dahl
Jelly Belly .... Smith
Kid Power .... Pfeffer
One-Eyed Cat .... Fox
Otis Spofford .... Cleary
Rabbit Hill .... Lawson
Sign of the Beaver .... Speare
Slave Dancer .... Fox
Stranger Came Ashore .... Hunter
There's a Bat in Bunk Five .... Danziger
Tuck Everlasting .... Babbit

GRADE LEVEL 8

Alas, Babylon .... Frank
Alive .... Read
The Autobiography of
   Miss Jane Pittman .... Gaines
The Boy Who Drank Too Much .... Green
Call It Courage .... Sperry
Clan of the Cave Bear .... Auel
Durango Street .... Bonham
Fifteen .... Cleary
Fox Running .... Knudson
Go Ask Alice .... Anonymous
Harry and Hortense at
   Hormone High .... Zindel
A Hero Ain't Nothin'
   but a Sandwich .... Childress
Homecoming .... Voigt
Ordinary People .... Guest
Rainbow Jordan .... Childress
Ransom .... Duncan
Rumble Fish .... Hinton
Sister of the Bride .... Cleary
Stranger with My Face .... Duncan
Tunnel Vision .... Arrick
War Between the Pitiful Teachers
   and the Splendid Kids .... Kiegel
West Side Story .... Shulman
Young Unicorns .... L'Engle

GRADE LEVEL 6

Can You Sue Your Parents
   for Malpractice? .... Danziger
Cay .... Taylor
Come Sing, Jimmy Jo .... Paterson
Dark Is Rising .... Cooper
Dear Lovey Heart,
   I Am Desperate .... Conford
Divorce Express .... Danziger
From the Mixed-Up Files of
   Mrs. Basil E. Frankweiler .... Konigsburg
Gentle Ben .... Morey
Ghost Belonged to Me .... Peck
The Girl Who Wanted a Boy .... Zindel
It's Not the End of the World .... Blume
Lottery Rose .... Hunt
Mary Jane Harper
   Cried Last Night .... Lee
Night Swimmers .... Danziger
One-Eyed Cat .... Fox
Sixteen: Short Stories by Outstanding
   Young Adult Writers .... Gallo, ed.
Sixth Grade Sleepover .... Blume
Solitary Blue .... Voigt
Something for Joey .... Peck
Summer Girls, Love Boys and
   Other Short Stories .... Mazer
Summer to Die .... Lowry
To Break the Silence .... Barrett, ed.
Trouble With Thirteen .... Blume
Undertaker's Gone Bananas .... Zindel
The Zucchini Warrior .... Korman

GRADE LEVEL 9

Beyond the Chocolate War .... Cormier
The Bloody Country .... Collier
Circle of Children .... MacCracken
The Contender .... Lipsyte
Dibs in Search of Self .... Axline
Durango Street .... Bonham
Flowers for Algernon .... Keyes
I Am the Cheese .... Cormier
I Never Loved Your Mind .... Zindel
I Never Promised
   You a Rose Garden .... Greenberg
Lovey: A Very Special Child .... MacCracken
Mr. & Mrs. Bo Jo Jones .... Head
Night .... Wiesel
A Night to Remember .... Lord
The President's Daughter .... White
Rainbow Jordan .... Childress
Something Wicked
   This Way Comes .... Bradbury
Watership Down .... Adams
The Wave .... Rhue
Wolf Rider .... Avi

Thematic Groupings

The titles grouped below lend themselves perfectly to in-depth units of study where students immerse themselves in high-interest themes or topics. These lists will be of special interest if you are involved in theme teaching in your middle school.

Family Relationships

GRADE LEVEL 6

All-of-a-Kind Family Downtown .... Taylor
And Condors Danced .... Snyder
Building Blocks .... Voigt
Charlie Pippin .... Boyd
Divorce Express .... Danziger
Dragonwings .... Yep
Edgar Allan .... Neufeld
The Endless Steppe .... Hautzig
Good-bye and Keep Cold .... Davis
A Hero Ain't Nothin'
   but a Sandwich .... Childress
In Summer Light .... Oneal
It's Not the End of the World .... Blume
A Jar of Dreams .... Uchida
Journey to America .... Levitin
Letters from Philippa .... Estern
Mom, the Wolfman, and Me .... Klein
The Moon by Night .... L'Engle
The Pistachio Prescription .... Danziger
Popcorn Days &Buttermilk Nights .... Paulsen
A Ring of Endless Light .... L'Engle
A River Ran Out of Eden .... Marshall
The Secret of the Indian .... Banks
Song of the Trees .... Taylor
Tracker .... Paulsen

Learning from the Past

GRADE LEVEL 6

After the Dancing Days .... Rostkowski
Alan and Naomi .... Levoy
Be Ever Hopeful Hannalee .... Beatty
The Bloody Country .... Collier
The Cage .... Sender
Charley Skedaddle .... Beatty
Constance .... Cove
Farewell to Manzanar .... Houston
Friedrich .... Richter
A Gathering of Days .... Blos
Grasshopper Summer .... Turner
Jump Ship to Freedom .... Collier and Collier
My Brother Sam Is Dead .... Collier
A Night to Remember .... Lord
The Night Journey .... Lasky
Prince and the Pauper .... Twain
Remembering the Good Times .... Peck
Rifles for Watie .... Keith
Sarah Bishop .... O'Dell
Snow Treasure .... McSwigan
Summer of My German Soldier .... Greene
Tuck Everlasting .... Babbitt
Turn Homeward, Hannalee .... Beatty
The Upstairs Room .... Reiss

Another Year Older

GRADE LEVEL 7

About David .... Pfeffer
Anything to Win .... Miklowitz
Banner in the Sky .... Ullman
The Butterfly Revolution .... Butler
Close Enough to Touch .... Peck
Cracker Jackson .... Byars
The Crossing .... Paulsen
The Egypt Game .... Snyder
Forever Friends .... Boyd
Friends Till the End .... Strasser
Good-bye Tomorrow .... Miklowitz
Henry Reed's Baby-Sitting Service .... Robertson
Hold Fast .... Major
Hoops .... Myers
I Am the Cheese .... Cormier
I Never Loved Your Mind .... Zindel
I Want to Keep My Baby .... Lee
The Island .... Paulsen
Midnight Hour Encores .... Brooks
A Night to Remember .... Lord
Notes for Another Life .... Bridgers
The Outsiders .... Hinton
Remembering the Good Times .... Peck
Tex .... Hinton
The Year Without Michael .... Pfeffer

Future/Fantasy

GRADE LEVEL 7

The Beggar Queen .... Alexander
The Curse of the Blue Figurine .... Bellairs
Dandelion Wine .... Bradbury
The Egypt Game .... Snyder
The Farthest Shore .... LeGuin
Freaky Friday .... Rodgers
Ghost Host .... Singer
The Girl Who Owned a City .... Nelson
The High King .... Alexander
The Kestrel .... Alexander
Many Waters .... L'Engle
A String in the Harp .... Bond
Summer of Fear .... Duncan
A Swiftly Tilting Planet .... L'Engle
The Third Eye .... Duncan
Time Machine .... Wells
Tombs of Atuan .... LeGuin
Unicorns in the Rain .... Cohen
The Voyage of the Dawn Treader .... Lewis
The War of the Worlds .... Wells
The White Mountains .... Christopher
A Wind in the Door .... L'Engle
Yukon Journey .... McLaughlin
Z for Zachariah .... O'Brien

Searching for Answers

GRADE LEVEL 8

Are You in the House Alone? .... Peck
Brian Piccolo: A Short Season .... Morris
A Circle of Children .... MacCracken
The Contender .... Lypsyte
Death Be Not Proud .... Gunther
Dibs in Search of Self .... Axline
Dinky Hocker Shoots Smack! .... Kerr
Flowers for Algernon .... Keyes
Goodbye, Paper Doll .... Snyder
A Hero Ain't Nothin'
   but a Sandwich .... Childress
Homecoming .... Voigt
Memory .... Mahy
My Darling, My Hamburger .... Zindel
Night Kites .... Kerr
The Ninth Issue .... Malmgren
Notes for Another Life .... Bridgers
Other Side of the Mountain .... Valens
The Pigman .... Zindel
Sarah T. .... Wagner
Say Goodnight, Gracie .... Deaver
Taming the Star Runner .... Hinton
Them That Glitter and
   Them That Don't .... Greene
Tunnel Vision .... Arrick
Waiting for the Rain .... Gordon

Out of This World

GRADE LEVEL 8

Against Infinity .... Benford
Anthem .... Rand
Beauty .... McKinley
Born into Light .... Jacobs
Childhood's End .... Clarke
Dragon's Blood .... Yolen
The El Dorado Adventure .... Alexander
Eva .... Dickinson
Fantastic Voyage .... Asimov
Farmer in the Sky .... Heinlein
The Hobbit .... Tolkien
Illustrated Man .... Bradbury
The Illyrian Adventure .... Alexander
Interstellar Pig .... Sleator
Martian Chronicles .... Bradbury
On the Beach .... Shute
Saturday the Twelfth of October .... Mazer
The Singers of Time .... Pohl & Williamson
Singularity .... Sleator
Star Wars .... Lucas
Tehanu .... LeGuin
2001: A Space Odyssey .... Clarke
Unicorns in the Rain .... Cohen
Westmark .... Alexander
A Wizard of Earthsea .... LeGuin

Multicultural Groupings

To help you and your students celebrate our rich multicultural heritage, we have also grouped important titles spanning our cultural spectrum. High-interest African-American, Asian-American, Hispanic-American, Jewish-American, and Native American titles are included. Use these lists to help you build a multicultural library in your class-room.

GRADE LEVEL 5

About the B'nai Bagels .... Konigsburg
All-of-a-Kind Family Downtown .... Taylor
Amos Fortune: Free Man .... Yates
Bright Shadow .... Thomas
The Buffalo Knife .... Steele
Drift .... Mayne
Fast Sam, Cool Clyde, and Stuff .... Myers
Felita .... Mohr
In the Year of the Boar and Jackie
   Robinson .... Lord
Ishi, Last of His Tribe .... Kroeber
A Jar of Dreams .... Uchida
Jesse Jackson: A Biography .... McKissack
Journey to America .... Levitin
Journey to Jo'burg .... Naidoo
The Lucky Stone .... Clifton
Martin Luther King: Peaceful
   Warrior .... Clayton
Racing the Sun .... Pitts
The Secret of Gumbo Grove .... Tate
Song of the Trees .... Taylor
The Story of George Washington
   Carver .... Moore
The Story of Junipero Serra: Brave
   Adventurer .... White
The Story of Roberto Clemente:
   All-Star Hero .... O'Connor
The Story of Sacajewea,
   Guide to Lewis & Clark .... Rowland
Who Is Carrie? .... Collier & Collier

GRADE LEVEL 6

And Now Miguel .... Kumgold
The Cay .... Taylor
The Defenders .... McGovern
Dragonwings .... Yep
Escape to Freedom .... Davis
Going Home .... Mohr
Julie of the Wolves .... George
Jump Ship to Freedom .... Collier & Collier
Listen Children .... Strickland, ed.
Ludie's Song .... Herlihy
Mary McLeod Bethune: Voice of
   Black Hope .... Meltzer
Moccasin Trail .... McGraw
My Name Is Not Angelica .... O'Dell
Roll of Thunder, Hear My Cry .... Taylor
Sadako and the Thousand Paper
   Cranes .... Coerr
The Sign of the Beaver .... Speare
Sing Down the Moon .... O'Dell
The Slave Dancer .... Fox
So Far From the Bamboo Grove .... Watkins
Sounder .... Armstrong
Sweet Whispers, Brother Rush .... Hamilton
A Way of His Own .... Dyer
Words by Heart .... Sebestyen

GRADE LEVEL 7

The Acorn People .... Jones
The Crossing .... Paulsen
Crystal .... Myers
Dogsong .... Paulsen
Edgar Allan .... Neufeld
Forbidden City - A Novel of Modern
   China .... Bell
Friedrich .... Richter
The Friends .... Guy
The Friendship & The Gold Cadillac .... Taylor
The Golden Pasture .... Thomas
Harriet Tubman: Conductor on the
   Underground Railroad .... Pety
A Hero Ain't Nothin' but a
   Sandwich .... Childress
Jump Ship to Freedom .... Collier & Collier
The Light in the Forest .... Richter
Lilies of the Field .... Barrett
Listen for the Fig Tree .... Mathis
Motown and Didi .... Myers
The Owl's Song .... Hale
Shadow of a Bull .... Wojciechowska
Sign of the Chrysanthemum .... Paterson
The Slave Dancer .... Fox
The Upstairs Room .... Reiss

GRADE LEVEL 8

Anne Frank: the Diary of a Young Girl .... Frank
Blue Tights .... Williams-Garcia
The Cage .... Sender
Carlota .... O'Dell
Chernowitz! .... Arrick
Child of the Owl .... Yep
Durango Street .... Bonham
The Education of Little Tree .... Carter
Farewell to Manzanar .... Houston
The Honorable Prison .... de Jenkins
I Heard the Owl Call My Name .... Craven
Kim/ Kimi .... Irwin
Long Journey Home .... Lester
Narrative of the Life of Frederick
   Douglass .... Douglass
The Outside Shot .... Myers
Rainbow Jordan .... Childress
A Thief in the Village: And Other
   Stories of Jamaica .... Berry
This Strange New Feeling .... Lester
Up From Slavery .... Washington
Waiting for the Rain .... Gordon
Walkabout .... Marshall
Young Fu of the Upper Yangtze .... Lewis

Read the best books first, or you may not have a chance to read them at all.
—Thoreau

Learning & Thinking Strategies

The learning and thinking strategies
on the following pages cover
a variety of topics often included
in a language program.

Active Learning

What can you do to promote active learning in your classroom?

There are any number of active learning approaches that you can work rather easily into your own classroom. Each one of them requires that you slightly modify your teaching to make it more student directed. Some of the most effective approaches are listed below:

(Each one of the following approaches can be used with *Write Source 2000* to promote active learning.)

- **Writing to Learn** (See pages 77-80 in this booklet and topics 006-010 in *Write Source 2000*.)
- **Minilessons** (See pages 93-110 in this booklet.)
- **Whole Language** (See pages 48-49 in this booklet.)
- **Personal Learning** (See personalized writing and learning ideas in *Write Source 2000*.)
- **Creative Thinking** (See pages 83-85 in this booklet.)
- **Cooperative Learning** (See 432-449 in *Write Source 2000*.)
- **Make a Writing and Reading Workshop Out of Your Classroom** (See pages 51-52 and 67-68 in this booklet.)

Active Learning . . .

- student plays active role
- student uses original sources and firsthand experiences, in addition to books
- every student becomes a source of information
- questions encourage students' ideas, attitudes, and beliefs
- questions require *an* answer, not a *right* answer
- variation in answers is expected
- more and higher-level thinking is required
- leads to appreciation of learning and builds desire to acquire and apply knowledge
- lets students develop how-to-learn strategies that will serve them for a lifetime
- builds self-esteem

Passive Learning . . .

- student plays passive role (usually sits quietly and listens)
- the text is THE source
- student uses text for nearly all "learning"
- nearly all questions require the *right* answer
- learning requires mainly lower-level thinking skills
- limits personal and imaginative thinking
- does not allow students to build how-to-learn strategies
- does nothing to build a student's self-esteem

Lots of Questions – A Few Answers
Writing to Learn . . .

Q. What exactly is "writing to learn"?

A. Writing to learn is a method of learning which helps students get more out of their course material. It is thinking on paper—thinking to discover connections, describe processes, express emerging understandings, raise questions, and find answers. It is a method which students can use in all subjects at all ages.

Q. What is the purpose of writing to learn?

A. The main purpose is better thinking and learning. (Better writing is a by-product.) This is why writing to learn is not just for English teachers.

Q. What makes writing to learn work?

A. Writing is uniquely suited to foster abstract thinking. The linearity of writing—one word after another—leads to more coherent and sustained thought than simply thinking or speaking. Also, when writing is used, all students can respond, including those who are reluctant to answer out loud.

Q. What are the advantages of writing to learn for students?

A. Writing to learn provides students with a way of learning, not just a set of facts. It forces students to personalize—to internalize—learning so that they understand better and remember longer. It also encourages higher-level thinking skills.

Q. What are the advantages for teachers?

A. Teachers using writing to learn will see learning, thinking, and writing improve among their students. They will also notice improved communication, rapport, and motivation as students become more independent and more actively involved in the learning process. Also, teachers will come to rely less and less on "writing to show learning," which needs to be graded.

Q. How do you go about beginning a writing-to-learn program?

A. First of all, there is no one "program" for writing to learn. Teachers can begin with the chapter "Writing to Learn" in *Write Source 2000*. After reading, writing, and discussing your way through this chapter, both students and teachers should have a good idea of what writing to learn is all about.

Then the teacher must select, from the wide variety of activities available, those which best suit the needs of their students. Once an activity is selected, it is very important that students understand they are "writing to learn," not "writing to show learning." If they understand that they are not writing simply to please their teacher, but to personalize and better understand information, you are on your way.

Q. Which writing-to-learn activities are good to begin with?

A. Learning logs, stop 'n' write, and admit slips (or exit slips) are excellent activities to begin a writing-to-learn program, although any of those listed on the next three pages will work just as well when matched to the right situation.

Writing-to-Learn Framework

PERSONAL WRITING

Recording	Learning Logs Class Minutes Active Note Taking
Gathering	Brainstorming First Thoughts Listing
Remembering	Focused Writing

SUBJECT WRITING

Describing	Observation Report
Reporting	5-W 1-H
Corresponding	Admit/Exit Slips Correspondence
Informing	Student Teachers How-To Writing
Searching and Researching	Interview/Survey Key Word Summing Up

CREATIVE WRITING

Translating	Bio-Poem
Inventing	Creative Definitions
Scripting	Dialogues Dramatic Scenarios Imaginary Conversations

REFLECTIVE WRITING

Persuading	Fact/Values List
Reviewing	Writing Groups
Analyzing	Instance Versions Stop 'n' Write Question of the Day

Writing-to-Learn Activities

The following activities can be used to promote writing to learn. Teachers (and students) should experiment with a variety of activities and then decide which ones best suit a particular course.

Active note taking: Students are asked to divide a page in half. On the left side, they are to record notes from their reading, and on the right side, they are to write comments or questions about the material they have read. This written dialogue makes note taking much more meaningful and provides students with material for class discussion. Among the comments students can make are the following:

* a **comment** on what memory or feeling a particular idea brings to mind,
* a **reaction** to a particular point which they strongly agree or disagree with,
* a **question** about a concept that confuses them,
* a **paraphrase** of a difficult or complex idea,
* a **discussion** of the importance or significance of the material,
* or a **response** to an idea that confirms or questions a particular belief.

Admit slips: Admit slips are brief pieces of writing (usually fit on half sheets of paper) which can be collected as "admission" to class. The teacher can read several aloud (without naming the writer) to help students focus on the day's lesson. Admit slips can be a summary of last night's reading, questions about class material, requests for teachers to review a particular point, or anything else students may have on their minds.

Bio-poems: Bio-poems enable students to synthesize learning because they must select precise language to fit into this form. (*NOTE:* Even though the bio-poem is set up to describe "characters," it can also be used to describe complex terms or concepts such as *photosynthesis, inflation,* etc.) Bio-poems encourage metaphorical and other higher-level thinking. A bio-poem follows this pattern:

Line 1. First name
Line 2. Four traits that describe the character
Line 3. Relative ("brother," "sister," "daughter," etc.) of _____
Line 4. Lover of _____ (list three things or people)
Line 5. Who feels_____ (three things)
Line 6. Who needs _____ (three things)
Line 7. Who fears _____ (three things)
Line 8. Who gives _____ (three things)
Line 9. Who would like to see _____ (three things)
Line 10. Resident of _____
Line 11. Last name

Brainstorming: Brainstorming (*list storming*) is writing done for the purpose of collecting as many ideas as possible on a particular topic. Students will come away with a variety of approaches which might be used to further develop a writing or discussion topic. In brainstorming, everything is written down, even if it seems at the time to be a weak or somewhat irrelevant idea.

Class minutes: One student is selected each day to keep minutes of the class lesson (including questions and comments) to be written up for the following class. That student can either read or distribute copies of the minutes at the start of the next class. Reading and correcting these minutes can serve as an excellent review, as well as a good listening exercise.

Clustering: Clustering is a special form of writing to learn which begins by placing a key word (nucleus word) in the center of the page. For example, suppose students were to write a paper on "responsibility" and what it means to them. *Responsibility* or *duty* would be an obvious nucleus word. Students would then record words which come to mind when they think of this word. They should record every word, circle it, and draw a line connecting it to the closest related word. (See the cluster example 035 in the handbook.)

Completions: By completing an open-ended sentence (which the teacher or other students provide) in as many ways as possible, students are pushed to look at a subject in many different ways. Writing completions also helps students focus their thinking on a particular lesson or concept.

Correspondence: One of the most valuable benefits of writing to learn is that it provides many opportunities for students to communicate with their teachers, often in a sincere, anonymous way. If no writing-to-learn activity seems to bring about this kind of open communication, teachers should set up a channel (suggestion box, mailbox, special reply notes, etc.) which encourages students to communicate freely and honestly.

Creative definitions: As in the game "Fictionary," students are asked to write out definitions for new words. Other students are then asked to figure out whether the definition is fact or fiction. When students are given the actual definition, there is a much better chance they will remember it.

Dialogues: Students create an imaginary dialogue between themselves and a character (a public or historical figure, for example) or between two characters. The dialogue will bring to life much of the information being studied about the life or times of the subject.

Dramatic scenarios: Writers are projected into a unit of study and asked to develop a scenario (plot) which can be played out in writing. If the unit is World War II, for example, students might put themselves in President Truman's shoes the day before he decided to drop the atomic bomb on Hiroshima, and create a scenario of what they think this dramatic time in history may have been like.

Exit slips: Students are asked to write a short piece at the end of class in which they summarize, evaluate, or question something about the day's lesson. Students must turn in their exit slips in order to leave the classroom. Teachers can use the exit slips as a way of assessing the success of the lesson and deciding what needs to be reviewed before going on with the next lesson.

Fact/values lists: When a new topic is being introduced, students write down everything they know to be a fact on the left side of their papers, and everything they "believe, feel, or suspect" about the topic on the right. Students will not only become immediately involved with the new topic, but sharing these lists is bound to provide some interesting introductory material for the whole class.

First thoughts: Students write or list their immediate impressions (or what they already know) about a topic they are preparing to study. These writings will help students focus on the task at hand, and they will serve as a point of reference to measure learning.

Focused writings: Writers are asked to concentrate on a single topic (or one particular aspect of a topic) and write nonstop for a certain amount of time. Like brainstorming, focused writing allows students to see how much they have to say on a particular topic, as well as how they might go about saying it.

Free writing: Students write nonstop on a particular subject for a certain amount of time. During a free writing, students often discover things about a particular subject they weren't aware they knew. They often discover connections or personal associations which were not at first obvious.

How-to writing: Students are asked to write instructions or directions on how to perform a certain task. This will help students both clarify and remember. Ideally, students would then be able to test their writing on someone who does not already know how the task is performed.

Instant versions: Students are given a composition assignment about a certain subject and then asked to pretend they are actually composing a final draft long before they are ready. Writing instant versions can help students clarify ideas and focus on "the big picture," as well as discover how much they know (or don't know) about the subject being studied.

Journals: Journals are places for students to keep their personal writings, including any of the writing-to-learn activities in this list. Often called "learning logs," journals allow students to record their impressions, questions, comments, discoveries, etc. about any subject, including the positive review given below by a student. (See "Journal Writing" in *Write Source 2000*.)

> *"This journal has got to be the best thing that's hit this chemistry class. For once the teacher has direct communication with every member of the class. . . . Thank you very much for all the help this journal has been to me."*

Key word: Students can be asked to write on a key word or concept connected to the lesson. By doing a focused writing in which they attempt to "define" a key word or "summarize" a concept, students are given an opportunity to consolidate and internalize the information being presented.

Learning logs: A learning log is a journal (notebook) in which students keep their notes, thoughts, and personal reactions to the subject. (See pages 30-31 in this booklet; also see "Guidelines for Keeping a Learning Log" in *Write Source 2000*.)

Listing: Freely listing ideas as they come to mind is another effective writing-to-learn activity. Students can begin with any idea related to the subject and simply list all the thoughts and details which come to mind. Listing can be very useful as a quick review or progress check.

Metacognition: Students are asked to write about their own thinking process, including where in the process they understood (or got lost) for the first time and how they went on from there. "Thinking about thinking" is especially useful in math and science.

Observation reports: The classic observation report has long been a staple in science labs. The objective is to collect data from close observation of objects, processes, and events. It is important to remember, however, that as with any writing-to-learn activity, an observation report should be written in language which allows students to personalize or internalize the information being written about.

Predicting: Students are stopped at a key point in a lesson and asked to write what they think will happen next. This works especially well with lessons which have a strong cause and effect relationship.

Question of the day: Writers are asked to respond to a question (often a "What if . . . ?" or "Why?") which is important to a clear understanding of the lesson or which prompts students to think beyond the obvious.

Stop 'n' write: At any point in a class discussion, students can be asked to stop and write. This will allow students a chance to evaluate their understanding of the topic, to reflect on what has been said, and to question anything which may be bothering them. These writings also help teachers assess how the lesson is progressing. (See "Predicting" above.)

Student teachers: An excellent way to encourage students to personalize or internalize class material is to have them construct their own mathematics word problems, science experiments, and discussion questions (which can be used for reviewing or testing). This is a great way to replace routine end-of-the-chapter or workbook questions with questions which students actually wonder about or feel are worth knowing.

Summing up: Students are asked to sum up what was covered in a particular lesson by writing about its importance, a possible result, a next step, or a general impression left with them.

Unsent letters: Letters can be written to any person on any topic related to the subject being studied. Unsent letters allow students to become personally involved with the subject matter and enable them to write about what they know (or don't know) to someone else, imagined or real.

Warm-ups: Students can be asked to write for the first five or ten minutes of class. The writing can be a question of the day, a free writing, a focused writing, or any other writing-to-learn activity which is appropriate. Warm-ups not only help students focus on the lesson at hand, but also give them a routine which helps break social contact at the beginning of each class.

Writing groups: Students can benefit greatly from working in groups. The writing which comes from a group discussion or brainstorming session can be either an individual or a collaborative effort. Group response to the writing can help students further clarify their thinking and writing. Group writing works especially well for quick summaries or short observation reports. (See "Group Advising" in *Write Source 2000*.)

For All Curriculums
Collaborative Learning

Collaborative (cooperative) learning is a powerful classroom strategy for both teachers and students. Collaborative learning is working together like we have always tried to do, but with new knowledge about group dynamics, borrowed largely from the areas of communication and psychology.

Obviously, you already know a lot about cooperative learning. You have been or are a member of many groups—families, sport teams, community groups, faculty committees, and so forth. Sometimes when we look at these groups, we tend to remember how ineffective they can be. It might be we feel we have a large body of knowledge about what NOT to do. This is okay. If nothing else, this is an incentive toward discovering what TO DO.

So what should a teacher who wants to use collaborative learning do?

First, we suggest that you experiment with collaborative learning before deciding if this classroom strategy is for you and your students. We provide three strategies you can use for this experimentation. The group skills you will want to work with are described in *Write Source 2000* (432-449).

While you are experimenting, keep these points in mind:

1. Collaborative learning allows teachers to move away from the front of the room and rely far less on lecturing.

2. Collaborative learning provides students with one of the most powerful ways to learn—verbalization.

3. Collaborative learning gives students more ownership of their learning and therefore motivates them to become better students.

Three Strategies That Work

The three strategies you can use for experimentation follow:

1. Tell/Retell Groups

Application: Any reading-to-learn activity
Recommended group size: 2 (3 in one group if you have an uneven number of students)
Group skills to emphasize: Listen actively (433), listen accurately (434), and offer words of encouragement (438).

STEP 1: One member reads a portion of the assigned material; the second member becomes an "active listener."

STEP 2: The second member tells what he/she heard; the first member becomes the "active listener." They decide *together* what the essential information is. (It's okay for them to look back at the reading material.)

STEP 3: Reverse roles and read the next portion.

2. Smart Groups

Application: Any reading-to-learn activity
Recommended group size: 2
Group skills to emphasize: Request help or clarification when needed (448), offer to explain or clarify (447), and never use put-downs (440).

STEP 1: Both students read assigned material. While reading, they put a faint check mark beside each paragraph they understand and a question mark beside any sentence, word, or paragraph they do not completely understand.

STEP 2: At each question mark, team members ask for help and clarification. If they both have questions, they try *together* to make sense of the material. If they both agree to seek outside help, they may consult another team or the teacher. If time allows, they may share what they remember about the passages they both understand.

"Three men helping one another will do as much as six men singly."
—Spanish Proverb

3. Up with Your Head Groups

Application: Checking comprehension and reviewing

Recommended group size: 4-5

Group skills to emphasize: Help a group reach a decision (449), learn how to disagree (444), and learn from disagreements (445).

STEP 1: Ask each student to number off within each group.

STEP 2: The teacher or a panel of students asks a question about the material that has been read.

STEP 3: Each group "puts their heads together" to make sure every member in their group knows an/the answer. When the question is an "open" question (one without a "correct" answer), the group reaches a consensus of opinion.

STEP 4: The questioner calls a number (1, 2, 3, 4, 5) and students with the corresponding number raise their hands to respond. When the question requires "an" answer, only one student need reply; but when the question is "open," a member from each group may reply.

What's the Next Step?

You will probably have many questions after experimenting. Questions such as these are common: "What is the teacher doing while students work?" "How do I assess student work?" "What happens when one group finishes before others?" "What is the best way to form groups?" "Are there more ways to use cooperative learning?" "How can I use cooperative learning in reading workshops? in writing workshops? to build vocabulary?"

Helpful HINT

Many valuable sources of information about collaborative learning are available to you. Ask other teachers, your curriculum director, and your department head to help you locate these sources. Also check with local colleges. Let your need be known.

Group Skills You Already Know

1. Use #3 voices.
   (A #1 voice would be a whisper; a #10 voice would be a scream.)

2. Move desks quietly.

3. Stay in your own space.

4. Sit so all members of a team can see everyone's face.

5. Introduce yourselves whenever necessary.

6. Take turns.

7. Call classmates by their names.

Teaching Thinking in the '90s

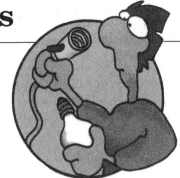

> *"Believe all students can think, not just the gifted ones. Let your students know that thinking is a goal. Create the right climate and model it."*
> —Arthur L. Costa

The market for teaching thinking was bullish at the end of the '80s, with articles regularly appearing in *Educational Leadership,* NCTE publications, and numerous other influential collections. Outstanding proponents of broader and better integrated approaches to thinking—leaders such as David Perkins, Art Costa, Richard Paul, Robin Fogarty, Barry Beyer, and others—were writing and speaking and inspiring teachers all over the country to "rethink" their classrooms.

Teacher Reaction

Many teachers have read and listened to what the experts have to say and, to some degree, have made thinking an important part of their curriculum.

Other teachers know that they should be challenging their students to think more critically and creatively, but they're not sure how to go about it. They wonder, in fact, if thinking is a skill which can be taught. Their concern is justified. Some educators say that effective thinking is a disposition or a temperament rather than a skill. Teachers are used to teaching skills, but teaching a disposition is another matter.

Then, of course, there are those teachers who wonder why so much fuss is being made about thinking. They say that their students have been thinking all along in their classrooms, and they're not about to change anything, thank you.

> *"In training a child to the activity of thought, above all things we must beware of what I will call 'inert ideas'* — that is to say, ideas that are merely received into the mind without being utilized, or tested, or thrown into fresh combination."*
> —Alfred North Whitehead

Creating a Thinking Climate in Your Classroom

For those of you who are ready to make your classrooms more "thinking oriented," we feel Arthur L. Costa offers the best advice in *Developing Minds* (ASCD, 1985). He suggests teachers teach **for thinking** (by creating the right classroom climate), **about thinking** (by helping students be more aware of their own thinking), and **of thinking** (by teaching thinking skills).

Teaching for Thinking

How can you create a thinking climate in your classroom? Read on and find out.

■ Personalize the learning in your classroom. Students will approach learning more thoughtfully when the subject matter means something to them personally. Common sense (plus plenty of studies) tells us students won't become thoughtfully involved in work that is not relevant to them personally. What does this mean to you? Don't teach out of a textbook. Use the students' own thoughts, feelings, and interests as starting points for thinking and learning.

 Take note of the emphasis on personalized learning in *Write Source 2000.* We provide you with plenty of ideas for personalized writing projects.

■ Promote activities that have heretofore been considered fillers: stories, poems, posters, letters, recipes, riddles, debates, discussions, etc. These are the types of activities that get students *actively* thinking and learning. (Basic skills activity sheets generally do not promote thinking.)

 Teachers interested in promoting thinking in their classrooms approach education as the acquisition of a wide range of experiences rather than the acquisition of information.

■ Engage your students in projects. Have them produce a class newspaper or magazine. Have them write and produce a play, a news show. Have them develop instructional manuals for skateboarding or bike repairing. There are any number of challenging thinking activities built in to long-range projects.

■ Involve students in collaborative learning. Collaboration is at the heart of learning outside of school. We learn how to ride, fish, bake, fix, etc. with the help of friends and family members. Collaborative learning gets people actively involved, gets them thinking, and gets them learning. It should be an important element in a thinking classroom. (See "Group Skills" in *Write Source 2000* for more information.)

Have your students work in writing groups. The give and take among students during writing projects promotes active thinking and better writing. (See "Group Advising" in *Write Source 2000* for guidelines. Also see "Peer Evaluation" in this booklet.)

■ Encourage open-ended, active learning in your classroom. Give your students every opportunity to explore, take risks, and make mistakes in your classroom. Ask them open-ended questions. Initiate role-playing activities, dramatic scenarios, discussions, and debates. Pose problems, search for alternatives, test hypotheses, and, generally, challenge your students to think and act for themselves

Have students write in a personal journal. There's no better way for them to explore their thoughts and feelings. (See "Journal Writing" in *Write Source 2000* for guidelines. Also see "Reading-Response Journals" in this booklet.)

Teaching About Thinking

Experts believe it's important that teachers help students think about their own thinking (metacognition). Focusing on one's thinking process leads to better thinking and learning. Here are some things you can do to help students metacogitate.

■ Explore with students how the brain works. Discuss left-brain thinking versus right-brain thinking. (See "Using Your Brain" in *Write Source 2000* for help.) Consider a discussion of artificial intelligence as well.

■ Select biographies of famous thinkers to share with your students.

■ Discuss with your students creative thinking, logical thinking, the connection between thinking and writing, the characteristics of effective thinkers, etc. (See the thinking section in *Write Source 2000* for help with this.)

■ Help students think about their own learning. Have them estimate how long an assignment will take. Have them determine what materials they will need to complete an assignment. Help them manage their work by breaking down challenging assignments into specific tasks. Help them find someone in class who can help them if they get stuck. Have them keep track of their progress during an extended project in a personal journal and so on.

■ Encourage students to take pride in their work. Remind them that their work is a reflection of their very own thinking. Have them evaluate their work upon its completion. They should consider what they liked or disliked about an assignment as well as what they succeeded at and what they need to work on. (See "Learning Logs" in *Write Source 2000* for more information.)

■ Remind students that it's all right to make mistakes, to get stuck, to reach dead ends. Give students an opportunity to talk or write about their thoughts and feelings when things aren't going well. Help them learn from these experiences.

■ Urge students to connect what they have already learned to new information. Also, take every opportunity to connect what they are learning to their personal lives. If you want to discuss **evaluating**, why not have students evaluate the merits of one pair of popular jeans versus another, of one popular pizza versus another, of one way of volunteering their services versus another?

Teaching of Thinking

A third component in a thinking classroom includes direct instruction of thinking skills. Here's how to work thinking skills into your curriculum.

■ Review a taxonomy of thinking skills, and select a limited number to emphasize throughout the year—perhaps one comprehension skill (summarizing), one analyzing skill (classifying), one synthesizing skill (predicting), and one evaluating skill (persuading). (See 330 in *Write Source 2000* for a list of thinking skills.)

Study a taxonomy of thinking skills carefully, and base your choice of skills to teach on your students' needs, your students' abilities, and your curriculum.

"The important thing is not so much that every child should be taught, as that every child should be given the wish to learn."
—**John Lubbock**

■ Produce your own activities for instruction or use thinking materials that are commercially produced. (*The Write Source 2000 Language Series* provides a number of problem-solving scenarios. See sample below.)

■ Arthur Costa suggests that these skills should not only be worked in to the general content area but taught independently in thinking activities. He suggests spending two or three hours per week in the direct teaching of thinking skills.

■ A thinking-skill lesson plan should follow this general format: Introduce the skill. (Find out what the students already know about it.) Demonstrate the skill. (Get your students actively involved in your "demonstration.") Have your students apply this skill in an activity. (Give them an opportunity to work in pairs.) Follow up with a discussion of the activity. (That is, have students reflect on the thinking they have done.)

■ Develop specific thinking activities which complement the "Thinking to Learn" section in *Write Source 2000*. You might

❑ have students identify and work through a problem to solve, an important decision to make, a difficult concept to understand, or an argument to build. (See 308.)

❑ have students refer to the thinking and writing chart (310) regularly for writing assignments.

❑ provide your students with a number of opportunities to focus on specific levels of thinking in writing assignments. (See 311-329.)

❑ give your students opportunities to think and write creatively. (See 331-342.)

❑ give them opportunities to think and write (and speak) logically. (See 343-355.)

What's the end result of making thinking an important part of your curriculum? Your students will become more tuned in to learning because they will become better equipped to think and learn for themselves. They will become active learners and make your classroom an exciting and stimulating place to be. And they will challenge you and make you more excited about teaching.

PROBLEM-SOLVING SCENARIO
INVENTING

Are You Game?

For twenty years Mr. Sporto and his gym classes have batted, blocked, and kicked with gusto. But twenty years is a long time, and Mr. Sporto is losing some of his enthusiasm. What he needs is a new game, a game that will renew the competitive fire in his eyes.

■ **Create a new game or sport for Mr. Sporto, and if it helps him forget football and baseball for a while, he just might use it next semester.** (Work in groups, if your teacher allows it.)

Talking to Learn

Many teachers have proven that talking to learn (verbalizing) is one of the most powerful ways for students to learn. These teachers have been designing and using a variety of effective ways for students to verbalize in classrooms because they know students will comprehend in a lasting way.

Some of the activities teachers have been using are very basic; others are more complex.

Basic Talking-to-Learn Activities

On page 81-82 in the collaborative learning section you will find three basic talking-to-learn designs which are appropriate for any content area. After experimenting with these basic talking techniques, students will be better prepared for more talking-to-learn activities in whole class or small group (four to five students) discussions.

More Talking-to-Learn Activities

1. Nerf Ball Discussion

Instead of merely calling on a student who raises his/her hand, toss a ball. When finished, that student can toss the ball to another student who has raised his hand or back to the teacher.

2. Talk and Yield Discussion

Use with either a whole class or small groups. The instructor picks the first speaker. When that speaker is finished, he/she picks the next speaker. There are no repeat speakers until everyone has had a turn, UNLESS the speaker who has not spoken volunteers to yield to a previous speaker who wants to make a point.

3. Read and Speak

Individual students read aloud a piece of writing which impresses them. This may be a page from a novel, a poem, a newspaper article, a scene from a short story or play. You may also have students read sentences or paragraphs from their own writing or another student's writing. After the reading the speaker explains why he thinks this piece is worthwhile, exciting, or well-done. Finally, he asks for questions from the class.

Using this method with textbooks can be especially effective. Students may choose the data in the text which most interested or surprised them, or they may introduce and read a portion from a piece of supplemental material that is germane to the topic. This could include current magazine and newspaper articles, novels, short stories, poems, letters, and even songs.

4. Talk and Record Sessions

(For evaluating group discussions)

When it is time for a discussion session, form groups of three to five students. Give each group a tape recorder, discussion guidelines and instructions, and plenty of time to develop their discussions. Upon completion of this group discussion, simply collect the recorded tapes, evaluate the work of each group, and during the next class period, share your observations with the class.

Why is talking to learn so powerful?

It is true that, at first, students will feel uncomfortable when vocalizing because they fear others will misinterpret what they say. It is also true that middle school students will get lost in their own argument and lose their train of thought. However, these are not reasons to avoid or abandon talking to learn; rather they are the very reasons to provide students with many opportunities to talk. Talking to learn gives speakers AND listeners a chance to practice real-life speaking and thinking skills while they gather content data and information.

How can the instructor insure a measure of success?

What can you do to make talking-to-learn work in your classroom?

1. Teach group skills. (See 432-449 in *Write Source 2000*. Require students to practice group skills when they work in groups.

2. Start with one of the basic talking-to-learn patterns. You might use one of these patterns to introduce your students to the information about group skills.

3. Schedule a formal conference with each group whenever a project is lengthy. In formal conferences you can model how talking together can be a productive process. Conferences are also a management tool. You will discover what the group is doing, who is contributing, who is practicing group skills, and what their needs are.

4. Make yourself available for informal sessions with small groups also.

For more about talking to learn see *Talking to Learn* available from National Council of Teachers of English, 1111 Kenyon Road, Urbana, IL 61801.

Acting to Learn

"Dramatic invention begins in play..."
—James Moffett and Betty Jane Wagner

At its core, drama is play. It is playful activity in which students use their bodies and senses to imagine people, animals, or objects—whatever roles they're acting out.

Because drama uses all the performer's senses, it is a useful tool for enhancing learning. The dramatic activities which follow will help your students use multiple senses to learn about literature and the writing process.

Characterization:

Joe Is an Ox—If a student has trouble clarifying a character's personality, ask the student to write a metaphor that compares the character to an animal: example—*Joe is an ox*. Ask the writer how ox-like Joe would walk, sit, or speak. Then have the writer watch as other students imitate Joe's bovine behavior by saying pieces of his dialogue, or doing bits of his action. Encourage the writer to watch and listen for details that may enhance his writing.

Hearing Dialogue—Help writers hear the rhythm of their dialogue by listening to other students read the dialogue. Remind readers to pay attention to a writer's punctuation, sentence structure, and word choice. Encourage writers to consider changing parts which sound unnatural, or inconsistent with the characters' personalities.

Listening Games: Ask students to remain seated at their desks and to lean forward, resting their heads.

Relax and Listen—Have students relax and listen carefully. In a quiet voice give these directions: "Close your eyes and breathe deeply, pulling the air from the bottom of your lungs. Let the weight of your body slowly settle on your desk, your chair, and on the floor. When you breathe, breathe deeply. Now listen to the sounds in this room. Identify five . . . five different sounds. [Pause ten seconds.] Listen to the sounds outside the room . . . identify three. [Pause ten seconds.] Listen to sounds outside the school . . . try to hear at least one. [Pause ten seconds.] Now, very slowly, and with your eyes still closed, sit up while I count to ten." Count slowly. When you reach ten, students will be sit-

ting. Ask them to open their eyes and talk about what they heard. (Because the exercise relaxes participants and sharpens their sensual awareness, it works well as a listening activity and as a prewriting activity.)

Listen and Add—Divide the class into groups of ten, and have each group form a circle. Ask a student in each circle to say a simple sentence that ends in a prepositional phrase: example—"I walked here *with my dog*." The person beside the speaker repeats the sentence, but adds an additional object of the preposition: "I walked here with my dog *and Uncle Pete*." The next person may say, "I walked here with my dog, Uncle Pete, *and Donald Duck*." The game continues until someone cannot repeat the list.

Plot Development:

Story Telling—To help a writer who gets stuck in the middle of a plot, ask three other students to join in a quick session of story telling. The writer reads the narrative as far as it goes, and each listener tells what he or she thinks will happen in the rest of the story. Invite the writer to use the ideas to complete the work.

Statues—If a writer cannot resolve the conflict in a scene, play the statue game. Cast the scene. Tell the characters to take their positions described in the scene and freeze like statues. Invite the writer to move the statues' heads, legs, or arms to create the precise picture of the scene. Ask the writer or other students to describe what is happening at this moment, and what might happen next. At this point you may call, "Curtain!" which cues the statues to come alive and improvise the action. Stop the scene as soon as actors lose focus. Invite the writer to use the actors' ideas.

Prewriting Exercises:

Concentration—Have students form two lines about six feet apart with each student in one line facing a partner in the other. Instruct line A to turn their backs on line B. Ask people in line B to change three things in their appearance: example—fasten a button, move a ring from one finger to another, and loosen a shoelace. Then ask students in line A to turn around, face their partners, and identify the three changes in the partner's appearance. Repeat the game.

The Storyteller—Have the class sit in a circle, and you stand in the middle. The first person you point to begins a story, "Once upon a time there was a . . ." Snap your fingers as you point to another student. Immediately, this person must continue the story, possibly saying, " . . . huge elephant with bright red ears. Now the elephant hated . . . " Again, snap your fingers while pointing to another student. The object of the game is to continue the story (1) without pausing, (2) without repeating what the previous speaker said, and (3) without changing the logic of the story. Continue the game until the story draws to a natural close. Students learn to concentrate—and they also generate ideas for their writing.

Responding to Literature:

Reader's Theater—To help students imagine how characters in a story may look or sound, do a reader's theatre performance. Prepare the script by making copies of the story, assigning a narrator to read the narrative parts, and assigning additional readers to read the characters' dialogue. Coach students to use their bodies and voices to suggest the personalities of their characters.

Imitating—Encourage students to assume the personality of a character by imitating how the character would sit, hold a pencil, comb his or her hair, roll up a sleeve, open a door, or say a line of dialogue. This activity helps students imagine characters in professional writing, or in their own writing.

Improvisation—Use improvisation to help students imagine what happens in a short story or novel. Start with a key half-page scene that includes no more than three characters. Read the scene with the class. Then cast the scene, and give the actors five minutes to develop an improvisation. Encourage them to act out what happens in the scene, but to improvise their own dialogue. Perform the piece, change details, and perform it again. Ask the class to compare the scene they read with the one they saw.

Pantomime Vocabulary Builder

The purpose of this activity is to build vocabulary and classification powers. Begin with a starter word such as *vehicle, emotion, clothing, machine, gesture, walk,* or *person,* and let the students brainstorm in two to four groups for synonyms for their word. Allow them to use a dictionary or thesaurus if necessary. Supply each group with a separate starter word and small pieces of paper to write

down each synonym (a "type" of vehicle, emotion, clothing, etc.). Then, in turn, each group shows one piece of paper to the teacher and pantomimes the word written on it. Perhaps the word is "strut," a synonym for "walk." (The teacher must announce the starter word.) The other groups each have a spokesperson to whom the members give their ideas. In turn, each group's spokesperson guesses the type of walk. If it is correct, that team gets a point. If it is not, another group has an opportunity to guess. If no group guesses correctly, the teacher may award the point to the presenting group, if the synonym was accurately presented, or give no point and tell the word. The second group now begins the process. Other starter words include *country, state, president, food, furniture, occupation, sports, dances, nouns, verbs, adjectives,* and *adverbs.*

Additional Sources:

Booth, David, and Charles Lundy. *Improvisation: Learning through Drama.* Toronto: Harcourt, 1985.

Chapman, Gerald. *Teaching Young Playwrights.* Portsmouth: Heinemann-Boynton/Cook, 1991.

Heinig, Ruth Beall. *Creative Drama for the Classroom Teacher.* Englewood Cliffs: Prentice Hall, 1993.

McCaslin, Nellie. *Creative Drama in the Classroom,* 5th ed. New York: Longman, 1990.

Moffett, James, and Betty Jane Wagner. *Student-Centered Language Arts, K-12,* Portsmouth: Heinemann-Boynton/Cook, 1992.

Building Vocabulary

What do we know about vocabulary development?

For one thing, we know there is a strong connection between a student's vocabulary and his or her reading ability. The same is true for a student's ability to listen, speak, and write. In fact, we now recognize that each person actually has four vocabularies, one each for reading, listening, speaking, and writing (listed here from largest to smallest). Although there is much overlap, students will always be able to recognize more words than they can produce. This is important to keep in mind as you develop a program of vocabulary development for your students.

Vocabulary development must also occur across the curriculum. Students must read, hear, speak, and write with the words they are attempting to learn in their classes. Anything less, and the words will not become part of their permanent "producing" vocabulary.

Existing studies tell us two things: (1) giving students lists of vocabulary words with little or no context is not an efficient way to teach vocabulary, and (2) students must be actively involved with the words they are attempting to learn.

Vocabulary-Building Strategies

The vocabulary-building strategies which follow have taken all of these points into consideration:

■ Previewing in Context

1. Select 5-6 words from a chapter or selection students are about to read.
2. Tell students to open their books to the page and paragraph in which each word is located. Have them find the word, read it in context, and try to figure out the meaning.
3. Ask students to write down what they think each word means.
4. Discuss possible meanings and arrive at the correct definition in this context.

■ Self-Collection

1. Students should set aside a portion of their journals or notebooks to collect personal vocabulary.
2. They may collect new and interesting words from any source, preferably outside of school.
3. Students should write journal entries that contain these new words and the contexts in which they were used.

4. Finally, students may analyze each word using its context, word parts, and dictionary definitions.

■ Prefix, Suffix, Root Study

1. Students should learn the most common prefixes, suffixes, and roots.
2. Students can be assigned 3-4 word parts each week for the entire year (see lists for each level on page 90).
3. Students can be given a number of strategies for learning these word parts:
   ❑ Assign students one word part a day (every day except Monday, perhaps). As you are taking roll, students can write out the word part, definition, a sample word, and a sentence using this word. Papers can then be exchanged and corrected.
   ❑ Ask students to brainstorm for word associations which will help them remember the meaning of each word part.
   ❑ Challenge students to combine the word parts they have studied into as many words as possible (perhaps in 5 minutes time, or as a challenge assignment for the next day). Special cards can also be used for this purpose:

Word Card

de re in	flex flect	ion or ible

   ❑ Require students to create "new" words using the word parts they have learned. To qualify, a new word should be one that makes sense and might actually be used if it were known to a large number of people.
   ❑ Invite students to share a "new" word and challenge the others to guess what it means and to write a sentence (or two or three) in which they use this word.
   ❑ Direct students to start a special section in their notebooks for word parts they come across in their other classes.

■ Context Clues Study

1. Students should read and discuss the context clues section of their *Write Source 2000* handbook.
2. Students should practice identifying the types of context clues as they use the previewing and self-collection techniques.

■ Other Forms of Word Study

1. **Special groups.** Students can be introduced to special groups of words found in computer language, music, politics, advertising, etc.

2. **Word play.** A certain amount of "word play" is essential to growth in vocabulary. Any type of word game will work so long as it is appropriate for the level of the students.

3. **Word-A-Day.** At the beginning of the class period, a word is printed on the board (a word that a student can use in his reading, listening, writing, and speaking vocabularies). As students enter the classroom, they immediately grab a dictionary and look up the word. As a class, students discuss the meaning and agree on a definition and a part of speech. They then use the word in a sentence, showing that they know what the word means and how to use it correctly.

    Each student jots down this information in a notebook. Each page is divided by a line drawn vertically at a point about one third of the width of the page. On the left side of this line, the word is written. On the right side of the line, the part of speech, definition, and sentence are written. This allows the student to cover the definitions by simply folding the paper.

    A written quiz can be given each Friday, covering the five words from the recent week and five words from any past weeks. The student must write the word in a sentence, proving again that he knows what the word means and how to use it.

Word Parts Study List

The following lists of word parts can be used as the basis of a vocabulary program for levels 6, 7, and 8.

LEVEL 6

Prefixes: anti (ant), bi (bis, bin), circum (circ), deca, di, ex (e, ec, ef), hemi (demi, semi), hex, il (ir, in, im), in (il, im), intro, mono, multi, non, penta, post, pre, quad, quint, re, self, sub, super (supr), tri, un, uni

Suffixes: able (ible), an (ian), ar (er, or), cide, cule (ling), en, ese, ess, ful, ion (sion, tion), ist, ity (ty), ize, less, ology, ward

Roots: anni (annu, enni), aster (astr), aud (aus), auto (aut), bibl, bio, breve, chrom, chron, cide, cise, cit, clud (clus, claus), corp, crat, cred, cycl (cyclo), dem, dent (dont), derm, dic (dict), domin, dorm, duc (duct), erg, fin, fix, flex (flect), form, fort (forc), fract (frag), geo, graph (gram), here (hes), hydr (hydro, hydra), ject, join (junct), jur (jus), juven, laut (lac, lot, lut), lic (licit), magn, mand, mania, meter, micro, migra, multi (multus), number (numer), omni, ortho, ped (pod),

phon, pop, port, prehend, punct, reg (recti), rupt, sci, scrib (script), serv, spec (spect, spic), sphere, tele, tempo, terra, therm, tract (tra), typ, uni, vid (vis), zo

LEVEL 7

Prefixes: ambi (amb), amphi, bene (bon), by, co (con, col, cor, com), contra (counter), dia, dis (dif), eu (ev), extra (extro), fore, homo, inter, mis, ob (of, op, oc), para, per, peri, poly, pro, se, syn (sym, sys, syl), trans (tra), ultra, under, vice

Suffixes: ance (ancy), ate, cian, ish, ism, ive, ly, ment, ness, some, tude

Roots: ag (agi, ig, act), anthrop, arch, aug (auc), cap (cip, cept), capit (capt), carn, cause (cuse, cus), civ, clam (claim), cord (cor, card), cosm, crea, cresc (cret, crease, cru), dura, dynam, equi, fac (fact, fic, fect), fer, fid (fide, feder), gam, gen, gest, grad (gress), grat, grav, hab (habit), hum (human), hypn, jud (judi, judic), leg, lit (liter), log (logo, ology), luc (lum, lus, lun), man, mar (mari, mer), medi, mega, mem, mit (miss), mob (mot, mov), mon, mori (mort, mors), nov, onym, oper, pac, pan, pater (patr), path (pathy), pend (pens, pond), phil, photo, plu (plur, plus), poli, portion, prim (prime), psych, put, salv (salu), sat (satis), scope, sen, sent (sens), sign (signi), sist (sta, stit, stet), solus, solv (solu), spir, spond (spons), string (strict), stru (struct), tact (tang, tag, tig, ting), test, tort (tors), vac, vert (vers), vict (vinc), voc

LEVEL 8

Prefixes: a (an), ab (abs, a), acro, ante, be, cata, cerebro, de, dys, epi, hyper, hypo, infra, intra, macro, mal, meta, miso, neo, oct, paleo, pseudo, retro, sex (sest)

Suffixes: asis (esis, osis), cy, dom, ee, ence (ency), et (ette), ice, ile, ine, ite, oid

Roots: acer (acid, acri), acu, ali (allo, alter), altus, am (amor), belli, calor, caus (caut), cognosc (gnosi), crit, cur (curs), cura, doc, don, dox, end (endo), fall (fals), fila (fili), flu (fluc, fluv), fum, gastro, germ, gloss (glot), glu (glo), greg, helio, hema (hemo), hetero, homo, ignis, later, levis, lith, liver (liber), loc (loco), loqu (locut), lude, matri (matro, matric), monstr (mist), morph, nasc (nat), neur, nom, nomen (nomin), nounce (nunci), nox (noc), pedo, pel (puls), phobia, plac (plais), plenus, pneuma (pneumon), pon (pos, pound), posse (potent), proto, que (qui), quies, ri (ridi, risi), rog (roga), sacr (sanc, secr), sangui, sed (sess, sid), sequ (secu, sue), simil (simul), somnus, soph, sume (sump), ten (tin, tain), tend (tent, tens), tom, tox, trib, tui (tuit, tut), turbo, vale (vali, valu), ven (vent), viv (vita, vivi), vol, volcan (vulcan), vor

Improving Student Spelling

"For better or worse, spelling places third in the American public's priorities for curriculum emphases. Reading takes first place, math second. Writing places eighth. In short, spelling is more important than what it is for . . . writing."
—**Donald Graves**

How should spelling be addressed in today's language arts classrooms if, in fact, the public gives it such a high priority? That question and more is explored in this discussion. What you'll find first is a list of instructional do's as reflected in the current research on spelling.

Direct Spelling Practices That Work

- Devoting approximately 10 minutes per day to direct instruction
- Presenting and studying words in short lists
- Drawing words primarily from one of the many master lists citing words frequently used by student and adult writers
- Studying the complete word rather than word parts or syllables
- Employing the pretest-study-test method of instruction
- Asking students to correct their own pretests
- Providing students with a strategy to learn how to spell new words (*Examine, pronounce, cover,* and *write*—repeated two or three times if needed—is one such strategy.)
- Linking spelling instruction, whenever possible, to the students' own writing (More on that later.)

Special Note: Teachers can refer to the commonly misspelled words listed in *Write Source 2000* (568-573) as a resource when developing weekly lists of words for instruction. Teachers (and/or students) should also add a few of their own words to the list—perhaps ones that students are often misspelling in their writing.

Spelling and Writing

There is really only one hard-and-fast rule to remember: Do not let students become overly concerned about the correctness of their spelling during the drafting stages of the writing process. This simple rule will do more than all the others to promote a healthy, realistic attitude toward spelling as it relates to writing.

Students should, however, be made to realize that before a piece of writing can be considered ready for publication, it must be as free of careless errors as possible. This includes spelling errors. Generally speaking, if students have worked long and hard, they know the content is good, and their classmates and instructor have shown an interest in the piece, they will want to spell all of the words correctly before they publish their work.

Helpful Hint: How can you help students improve their spelling skills as they work on their writing? First, you can ask them to circle which words are spelled incorrectly in their work before they ready a draft for publication. If a student needs more direction, you can write at the top of the paper, "There are four words misspelled," and let the student attempt to find the four words.

Next, teach your students the various systems they can use to correct a misspelling. These should include using a poor speller's dictionary, compiling a personal dictionary of frequently misspelled words, utilizing computer spell checkers, and having access to the classroom spelling expert.

Is Spelling Still Important?

You may hear from middle-school students, "Why do I have to learn to spell when I can use a computer spell checker?" The truth of the matter is that there is still a very good reason for learning to spell, especially the words a writer uses again and again. A writer who can spell can put the words behind him or her and focus on more important matters like exploring and shaping ideas. Also, once a spell checker identifies a misspelling, a writer still has to know how to correct the error.

Special Note: The *Write Source 2000 Language Series* provides a framework for an easy-to-implement and timely spelling program for middle-school teachers.

Professional Titles for Language Arts and English Teachers

We highly recommend the following titles on writing, reading, and teaching for middle-school and high-school language arts teachers. All titles are Heinemann-Boynton/Cook publications, unless otherwise indicated.

In the Middle
Nancie Atwell

Ms. Atwell, a former middle-school language arts teacher in Booth Bay, Maine, details her successful middle-school writing and reading workshops. *In the Middle* contains a clear discussion of workshop procedures, practical advice, techniques for conferring with writers and readers, and many examples of student writing. All teachers of writing and reading should share in Ms. Atwell's experiences.

Side By Side: Essays on Teaching to Learn
Nancie Atwell

Each essay in this book challenges programs and methods that distance teachers from students and distort the process of writing and reading. Each essay also helps teachers become more active and involved participants in writing and learning. *Side By Side* is an excellent companion piece to *In the Middle*.

Seeking Diversity: Language Arts with Adolescents
Linda Rief

Ms. Rief, an eighth-grade teacher in Durham, New Hampshire, presents an enlightening and stimulating look at her classroom where "the intellectual and emotional needs of her students are the crux of her curriculum." Students and the teacher alike thrive in Ms. Rief's classroom. This book is must reading for all teachers in the middle grades and beyond.

Living Between the Lines
Lucy McCormick Calkins with Shelley Harwayne

This book invites teachers to bring new life to the reading-writing workshop and challenges them to rethink the teaching of reading and writing. *Living Between the Lines* includes chapters on keeping a writer's notebook, on introducing wonderful literature, and on experimenting with new workshop ideas.

The Reading/Writing Teacher's Companion
Donald H. Graves

This series of short volumes, by the author of *Writer: Teachers and Children at Work*, includes *Investigate Nonfiction, Experiment with Fiction, Discover Your Own Literacy, Build a Literate Classroom,* and *Explore Poetry*.

Active Voice: A Writing Program Across the Curriculum
James Moffett

According to many writing experts, this book offers the best sequence of compositions available in print. The forms of writing cataloged in *Write Source 2000* reflect Moffett's approach to writing instruction. (*Active Voice I & II* provide the "Moffett" sequence plus student models for grades 4-6 and 7-9.)

Authors' Insights: Turning Teenagers into Readers & Writers
Donald R. Gallo, editor

The distinguished voices in young adult literature—from Norma Fox Mazer to Robert Cormier—discuss literature and writing, hitting upon many key issues related to current theory and practice. *Authors' Insights* is a book that will help teachers turn reluctant readers into avid readers.

Mind Matters: Teaching for Thinking
Dan Kirby and Carol Kuykendall

Mind Matters discusses a number of important questions about thinking instruction. One fundamental question is at the core of the book: How can teachers help students develop "thoughtful" habits of the mind? The thinking habits of artists, naturalists, inventors, and anthropologists are explored.

Writers in Training
Rebekah Caplan

Teachers need this resource if their students do more "telling" than "showing" in their writing. In addition to helping teachers establish a program of "showing" writing activities, *Writers in Training* provides guidelines for comparing and contrasting, developing argumentative essays, doing "I-search" papers, and employing a variety of revising techniques. (Available through Dale Seymour Publications.)

Minilessons

The following pages contain
over 70 minilessons which you and
your students can use with your
Write Source 2000 handbooks.

Minilessons

Minilessons can transform any classroom into an active learning environment. (We define a minilesson as anything that lasts about 10 minutes and covers a single idea or a basic core of knowledge.) Minilessons can be delivered from the front of the room and include the entire class. They can also be individualized or worked into cooperative learning groups. Ideally, each lesson will address a particular need—a need some students are experiencing right now. This makes learning much more meaningful and successful.

Minilessons work very well in the writing workshop classroom. Those people who are "stuck" can be pulled together for 10 minutes each day until they solve their problem. Perhaps one group of students has a need to know how to punctuate dialogue because they are writing stories. Another group of students may need information and practice combining sentences. And still another group may need help with forming possessives. All this (and more) can be scheduled within one class period. The diverse needs of students can be met by teaching them the skills they need . . . when they need to learn them.

The first several pages of the minilessons which follow focus on "The Yellow Pages" section in *Write Source 2000*. They address aspects of punctuation, spelling, usage, grammar, and sentence structure. The remaining pages cover a variety of topics from throughout the handbook. (The suggested level for each minilesson is in parentheses.)

Stop it! ....*Using Periods* (6)

■ Study the rules in "The Yellow Pages" for using periods (**460-463**).
  WRITE a sentence about something that came to a dead stop—a train, a game, a popcorn popper, or whatever.
  In your sentence, SHOW all four uses of the period: after an initial, as a decimal point, at the end of a sentence, and after an abbreviation. (Be inventive!)

Broken Reply ....*Using Ellipses* (7)

■ Study the guidelines for using ellipses (**465-467**).
  REMEMBER (or imagine) a time when you broke something valuable that belonged to someone else.
  SUPPOSE the owner asks, in pain or in anger, "How did *this* happen?"
  WRITE a broken reply, using ellipses correctly to show pauses and missing words.

Cold Serial ....*Commas in a Series* (8)

■ Study the guidelines for using commas to separate items in a series (**469**).
  SUPPOSE you won a free, round-trip plane ticket to Antarctica but you may pack only one small suitcase.
  WRITE a complete sentence which lists everything you pack for your f-r-r-r-reezing journey.
  USE commas correctly to separate items in the series.

Sandy Claws ....*Punctuating Clauses and Phrases* (6)

■ Study the guidelines for using commas to separate clauses and phrases from the rest of the sentence (**477, 478, 480 & 481, 482**).
    SUPPOSE you brought a rambunctious dog to the beach and it created a major ruckus—ran away with swimsuits, kicked sand into coolers, etc.
    WRITE a paragraph about what happened at the beach.
    MAKE each sentence demonstrate a different point about the use of commas to separate clauses and phrases.
    WRITE another paragraph explaining what each one of your sentences demonstrates.

Keeku! Keeku! ....*Using Semicolons* (7)

■ Study the guidelines for using semicolons (**484-487**).
    READ "Fashionation" (**141**).
    FIND two sentences which use semicolons; REWRITE the independent clauses in them as separate sentences.
    FIND two other pairs of sentences that could be joined with a semicolon; JOIN them, punctuating correctly.

Lower the flow. ....*Using Colons* (8)

■ Study the guidelines for using colons to introduce a list (**493**). Pay special attention to the samples.
    THINK UP three new ways either to control styrofoam waste or to conserve water.
    WRITE an *incorrectly punctuated* sentence containing a list of your three items.
    TRADE papers with a partner.
    WRITE a correct version of your partner's sentence using a colon properly to introduce the items in a series.

Hyphen a Good Time...................*Using Commas and Hyphens* (8)

■ Quickly review the guidelines for both commas (**468-482**) and hyphens (**498-505**).
    PUNCTUATE the following sentence correctly so it makes sense:
    Two thirds of those fat bellied gap toothed chew spittin' practically brain fried motorcycle maniacs had five mile long prison records.

So to Speak ....*Using Quotation Marks* (7)

■ Study guideline **516** for using quotation marks.
    THINK of a distinctive slang word which one of your friends always uses.
    WRITE a sentence about your friend, using the word in a special way.
    USE quotation marks properly to draw attention to the special use.

Pssst! .... *Using Quotation Marks* **(7)**

■ Study the guidelines for using double and single quotation marks (**511-515**).
REMEMBER something you said earlier today (or earlier this year).
IMAGINE you overhear two people gossiping about you. (Where are they? How do they
know you? What is their attitude toward you?) One is telling the other what you said,
using your exact words.
WRITE down their conversation exactly, using double and single quotation marks
correctly.

Enchanted, I'm sure. .... *Using Parentheses* **(8)**

■ You know how sometimes you *say* one thing and *think* another?
STUDY the guidelines for using parentheses (**532**).
THINK of a time when you met somebody new and said all the polite things.
WRITE a paragraph showing what you said, but in parentheses write down what you
really thought.

Shopping with the Biggies .... *Capitalization* **(6)**

■ Study the rules for capitalization (**533-546**).
LIST three or four quite different famous people.
For each famous person, SUPPOSE that he or she went shopping for food, brand name
clothes, etc.
WRITE each person's shopping list *without* any capital letters.
TRADE papers with a partner and capitalize correctly.
CHECK your partner's work.

Double Vision .... *Forming Plural Nouns* **(7)**

■ Study the guidelines for forming plural nouns (**547-554**).
SUPPOSE you were attending a national convention of twins; you and your twin are
talking with another pair of twins about what a pain it is to have to buy two of
everything.
WRITE your conversation in the form of a play script (see **260** for a model), using as many
different kinds of plurals as you can.

Digital Readout .... *Writing Numbers* **(6)**

■ Study the rules for writing numbers correctly (**558-562**).
REWRITE the following sentence correctly:
8 or nine of the twenty-6 seniors, or about 2 point six percent of the entire high school
population, had pledged to read 200 200-page books by July Four, Two Thousand A.D.
TRADE papers with a partner and critique your revisions.

E Before I ....*Spelling* (6)

■ Study the exceptions to the "i before e" rule in **564**.
COMPOSE your own sentence containing all of these exceptions: *their, height, counterfeit, foreign,* and *heir.* (Good luck!)

Bad Spellers' Dictionary ....*Spelling* (8)

■ Note "The Yellow Pages Guide to Improved Spelling" (**568-573**).
COMPILE a *Bad Spellers' Dictionary.*
First, COLLECT all the words you usually misspell.
Second, LIST the words the way you usually spell them (the wrong way).
Finally, after each wrong spelling, SHOW the correct spelling.
GIVE your *Bad Spellers' Dictionary* to some poor, needy soul—or keep it for yourself and keep adding to it.

Double Trouble ....*Using the Right Word* (8)

■ Study "The Yellow Pages Guide to Using the Right Word" (**574-694**) until you find a number of pairs of words which you usually mix up.
COPY the model "cumulative" sentence in **113** and study how it's made.
WRITE a sentence with a similar structure but on a topic you choose.
In your sentence, USE at least two words wrongly (for example, use "principle" for "principal" and "you're" for "your").
SWITCH papers with a friend. INVITE your friend to enjoy your cumulative sentence, and CHALLENGE him or her to find and correct the wrongly used words.

Door Jam .... *Spotting Subjects and Predicates* (7)

■ Study the sections on subjects and predicates (**696-705**).
READ the story in section **401** about the girl who lost her fingernail playing "chicken."
LIST on a separate sheet the simple subject and simple predicate in each sentence.
PUT a star next to the five most effective subjects and predicates.

Seeing Spots ....*Independent and Dependent Clauses* (6)

■ Study the guidelines for independent and dependent clauses (**710**).
Study the Braille alphabet in **799**.
WRITE a complex sentence (a sentence with one independent clause and at least one dependent clause) in *Braille.*
Special Challenge: Translate your sentence into Morse code (**800**) or cuneiform (**801**).

Blind Tom...*Types of Sentences* (8)

■ Study the different types of sentences in **711-714**.
READ the "phase biography" about Blind Tom (**156**).
On a separate sheet of paper, WRITE numbers 1 through 11.
MARK each sentence in "Blind Tom" according to type: S = Simple, Cx = Complex,
   Cd = Compound, CC = Compound-Complex.
DECIDE which type of sentence the writer uses most.

The Four Stooges on Venus ....*Kinds of Sentences* (7)

■ Study the four different kinds of sentences described in **715-718**.
CREATE four characters—four "stooges"—one who speaks only in *declarative* sentences,
   another only in *interrogatives*, another only in *imperatives*, another only in *exclamations*.
WRITE a short, funny radio drama about the "Four Stooges" as they step out of their
   Venusian Landing Vehicle (VLV) onto a weird new planet. (Keep each of the stooges
   in character.)
HINT: You'll have more to work with if you first study what scientists already know
   about the atmosphere on Venus.

Pandora's Box ....*Forming Possessives* (6)

■ Review the instructions for forming possessive nouns (**731**) and possessive pronouns (**741**)
and for using apostrophes to punctuate singular and plural possessive nouns (**522-523**).
IMAGINE that three teenage brothers and sisters (you may decide the combination)
   stumble across a box full of their childhood toys. They disagree violently about what
   toy belongs to whom.
WRITE out their excited (maybe angry, maybe funny) conversation—use play-script
   format (see **260**) if you wish.
PUT all possessive nouns and pronouns—correctly punctuated, of course—in ALL CAPS.

Lost and Found (I) ....*Identifying Types of Nouns* (7)

■ Study the definitions and examples of types of nouns in **719-724**.
On a sheet of paper, MAKE three headings: "Concrete Nouns," "Abstract Nouns," and
   "Collective Nouns."
READ the fascinating biography of Francis Ann Slocum in section **157**.
LIST all the concrete nouns in the biography under the proper heading; do the same for
   abstract and collective nouns.
PLACE a "c" in parentheses after the word if it is a common noun and a "p" if it is proper.

Lost and
Found (II) .... *Identifying Pronouns and Antecedents* (7)

■ Review personal pronouns and antecedents in **733-735**.
READ once again the story of Francis Slocum's life among the Miami Indians (**157**).
LIST all the personal pronouns you can find.
After each pronoun, add a dash and write the antecedent (if you can find one).

And on Your Left .... *Kinds of Pronouns* (7)

■ Review the "Other Types of Pronouns" (besides personal pronouns) in **743-748**; notice the helpful chart after **748**.
Now SUPPOSE you landed a job as a tour guide who has to show international visitors all the fascinating sights in your own bedroom. It's your first day of work and you need to practice.
WRITE down a first draft of your spiel.
USE at least one of each kind of pronoun—relative, demonstrative, interrogative, intensive, reflexive, and indefinite.
TRADE papers with someone and challenge him or her to find an example of each different kind of pronoun.

I get a kick out of this. .... *Active and Passive Verbs* (6)

■ Review the definitions of active and passive voice in verbs (**753-754**).
CHOOSE a sport which involves hitting or kicking a ball.
WRITE a paragraph describing a moment of intense action in that sport from the point of view of one of the players; USE active verbs.
REWRITE the paragraph, describing the same action from the point of view of the ball; USE passive verbs.

Munchies .... *Verb Tenses* (8)

■ Review the sections on verb tenses (**755-760**)—present, past, future, present perfect, past perfect, and future perfect.
THINK about the food you eat.
WRITE sentences about three day's worth of meals and snacks.
START your sentences with the following phrases and USE the appropriate verb tense:
By yesterday noon,
Yesterday,
Since yesterday,
Today,
Tomorrow,
Already by noon tomorrow,

All the Right Parts............*Principal Parts of Irregular Verbs* (8)

■ Study the chart of "Common Irregular Verbs and Their Principal Parts" until you know all the verb forms.

    MAKE your own set of flash cards.

    PUT the present tense form of a verb on one side; PUT the past tense and past participle on the other side.

    TRY to stump your neighbor; ASK your neighbor to make up sentences using the three principal parts correctly.

Weird Objects: *Transitive Verbs; Direct and Indirect Objects* (8)

■ Study the sections on "Transitive Verbs" (**762**), "Direct Object" (**763**), and "Indirect Object" (**764**).

    MAKE UP ten weird sentences using your own combinations from the following lists:

VERBS	INDIRECT OBJECTS	DIRECT OBJECTS
force-fed	ostrich	sandwich
tossed	catcher's mitt	medicine ball
handed	piano tuner	love letter
left	carburetor	BB
floated	jellyfish	jungle gym

"To Be" or Not "To Be" ....*Intransitive Verbs* (8)

■ FIND and JOT DOWN at least two intransitive verbs in the one-paragraph book review of *Tom Sawyer* (**190**).

For a harder challenge, FIND and JOT DOWN three intransitive verbs in the multi-paragraph book review of *Prince Caspian* (**191**).

    Caution: Don't call a verb intransitive if it is in the passive voice (**754, 762**), or if it has a gerund (**768**) or an infinitive (**770**) or a noun phrase (**709**) for an object.

Beyond Awesome, Different, and Cool ....*Degrees of Adjectives and Adverbs* (7)

■ Study the positive, comparative, and superlative forms of adjectives (**779-784**) and adverbs (**787**).

    THINK of three different things to compare—three roller coasters, three movies, three flavors of pizza, etc.—where one seems good, another better, and the third best (or bad, worse, and worst).

    SUPPOSE one friend describes the three things as "awesome, more awesome, and most awesome"; another retorts, "No man, they are cool, cooler, and coolest!"

    Not satisfied, you WRITE your own critique of the three.

    USE the three degrees of adjectives and adverbs effectively in your critique.

Club Ed .... *Journal Writing* (7)

■ Wonder how to get started writing in a journal? Why not look over the advice on starting a journal in section **131-132**? Check out the idea of writing in a learning log (more on that in **409**). Then,

READ the opening pages of *Write Source 2000*, "An Invitation to Learning" (**001-002**). Focus on what the writer means by "Club Ed."

WRITE in your journal whatever thoughts come to your mind about learning that you experience outside the classroom. Don't settle for the first thoughts that pop up. Keep digging. How many kinds of things do you learn "on the outside"? How is learning outside of school different from learning in school? What would learning be like inside school, if you had *your* way?

Sprints and Marathons .... *Managing Your Time* (6)

■ Under the heading "Managing Your Time" (**452**), pay special attention to the point labeled "Turn big jobs into smaller jobs."

THINK of a job you must do (now or later) which will take more than one day to accomplish.

BREAK that job down into smaller jobs that will each take no more than one hour.

LIST all the smaller jobs under the heading of the one big task. GROUP them under subheadings if that will help.

Everybody, shut up! .... *Improving Group Skills* (8)

■ Suppose you are the secretary for your school's student council—maybe you really are! Suppose your group, like many groups, is having a hard time getting anything accomplished because everybody talks and nobody listens.

STUDY carefully the guidelines for "Group Skills" in sections **432-449**.

Quickly REVIEW the guidelines for writing summaries (**184-186**).

WRITE a solid summary of "Group Skills" to submit to your student council as a recommendation.

It was a dark and stormy night. .... *Writing Openings* (7)

■ Think of a story from your life that you've been saving to tell somebody.

READ section **019**, "Writing an Opening or Lead Paragraph."

WRITE your most interesting opening paragraph for your story.

GIVE your opening paragraph to someone else to read.

ASK that person to write down whatever questions the opening makes them want answered.

REWRITE the opening so that it raises even better questions.

GIVE your opening to your reader again and repeat the process.

Off the Beaten Path .... *Offbeat Questions* (7)

■ Get a feel for the "Offbeat" or "Unstructured" questions in **038**.
   Then WRITE an "offbeat" question (and an offbeat answer) about a certain place, object, or event.
   WRITE two more offbeat questions and answers about your subject; SHARE your work with a classmate.

Twenty-Five Steps .... *"Found" Writing Ideas* (7)

■ Look over section **033**, "Creating a Writing 'SourceBank'," and pay special attention to the subsection " 'Found' Writing Ideas."
   JUMP in the air and SPIN (with your teacher's permission). Don't move your feet when you land.
   TAKE 25 steps in the direction your feet are pointing—of course, you should stop if you come to a wall or any other immovable object.
   WRITE fast and furiously about whatever you see from there or whatever comes to your mind.

Fanning Out ....*Clustering* (6)

■ Choose one of the topics from the "Essentials of Life Checklist" in **036**.
   USE that word as the "nucleus word" for a cluster that you create.
   FOLLOW the directions for clustering in **035**.
   At the end of your clustering, CHOOSE the one word you've written that would make the most interesting topic for writing.
   WRITE FREELY about your topic for 5-10 minutes in class or on your own time.

Whose Pants These Are .... *Imitating a Poem* (8)

■ Read and appreciate the poem "Stopping by Woods on a Snowy Evening" by Robert Frost (**229**). Pay attention to the line length, the rhyme scheme, the rhythm, the subject, the word choice, the mood, etc.
   WRITE a "parody" (a playfully twisted imitation) of Frost's poem. First,
   CHANGE the word "woods" in the first line to any other word that makes some kind of sense (pants, gloves, car, house, cheese, pen, etc.).
   ALTER the rest of the first line so that it fits your new word but still sounds "sort of" like Frost.
   FINISH the poem in the same way. Don't be afraid to let your new poem take off on its own if it "wants" to.

Goal to Go .... *Goal Setting* (7)

■ In the section on "Individual Skills" (**450-457**), read with special care about "Setting Goals" (**450-451**). On paper,

WRITE DOWN one goal for next hour.
"   "   "   " for tonight.
"   "   "   " for tomorrow.
"   "   "   " for next week.
"   "   "   " for next year.
"   "   "   " for your life.

Alphabet Cluster .... *Selecting a Writing Subject* (8)

■ Read the directions for "Clustering" under "Selecting a Writing Subject" (**035**).
ASK your nearest neighbor to pick any letter of the alphabet.
WRITE DOWN a word that comes to mind starting with that letter.
USE that word as the "nucleus word" for a cluster.
DEVELOP your cluster until you run out of ideas.
PICK an idea from your cluster and
WRITE about it for 8 minutes.

Byte Into This .... *Computers and Writing* (8)

■ Remind yourself of the steps involved in personal research and in writing a "research story" (**265-270**). Then read the short section on "Computers and Writing" (**287**). If you know how to use a computer, then do this personal research project:

THINK of two people you know about equally well. You must be interested enough in them to write character sketches about them (see **159-165**).
WRITE one character sketch in pencil or pen.
WRITE the second character sketch on a computer. Afterward,
RATE the two sketches on 1) time each took to write, 2) amount of prewriting, 3) length, 4) amount of drafting and revising, and 5) quality of writing.
WRITE UP your experience in a personal research report.

Butcher, Baker, Candlestick Maker ..*Ideas for Short Stories* (8)

■ Read the hilarious and insightful interview with the story writer Bob Kann (**239**). Then look over the "Essentials of Life Checklist" (**036**).

CHOOSE one "essential of life" from each of the three columns.
MAKE UP three characters, each one associated with one of your three "essentials of life."
BEGIN to write a story in which all three characters are forced to interact. WRITE the story to *find out* what they do.
WRITE fast and furiously for 5-8 minutes. Then MAKE NOTES to help you finish the story later.

Dear Mr. Zzyzz: .... *Writing a Business Letter* (8)

■ Study the instructions for writing a business letter (**203-214**). Memorize the format called "Semiblock" (**204**). Next,

GO THROUGH the list of "Writing Topics" in section **040** and pick any topic that especially interests you. Next,

PICK any name at random from your city's telephone book. Next,

WRITE a business letter in semiblock form asking the person you've picked if he or she has any special information about your topic.

Between Covers .... *Parts of a Book* (7)

■ Review the description of "Parts of a Book" in section **301**.

STUDY the parts and organization of *Write Source 2000*.

PUT a check mark in section **301** by each part that *Write Source 2000* contains.

LIST other parts of *Write Source 2000* that are not mentioned in **301**.

Why We Hiccup .... *Exercises in Style* (6)

■ Under "Writing Topics" (**040**), notice the prompts under the subheading "Explaining . . . the causes of . . . ."

CHOOSE one of the topics.

PRETEND you are a kindergartner and write an explanation of the cause of, say, a tornado or a hiccup.

Now SWITCH. PRETEND you are an 80-year-old man or woman; EXPLAIN the causes of the same thing from that point of view.

Sharpened Ax Today .... *Exercises in Style* (8)

■ Browse around in the sections on "Styling Sentences" (**109-111**).

IMAGINE you are somebody quite different from who you are: an astronaut, a Miss America candidate, an ax murderer, a cab driver, a dolphin trainer, etc.

WRITE one page of that person's daily diary in the style you imagine that person would have. MAKE the style clearly different from your own.

Through Different Lenses ....*Writing About Experiences* (7)

■ Review the sections on "Writing About Experiences" (**144-149**).
CHOOSE an experience you've always wanted to tell about.
TURN to the list of "Writing Forms" in section **041**.
CHOOSE one writing form from each of the four categories: personal writing, creative writing, subject writing, and persuasive writing.
WRITE four versions of your experience, one in each different form.

My Partner, 'Tis of Thee ....*Writing Biography* (6)

■ Brush up on techniques of interviewing (see section **405-407**).
STUDY the directions for writing a "Bio-Poem" (**158**).
CHOOSE a partner from the class.
INTERVIEW your partner until you have found out enough information to complete a "bio-poem."
WRITE a bio-poem about your partner and give it to him or her as a gift.

Eyes Like Meteors ....*Writing a Character Sketch* (8)

■ Read through the sections on writing a "Character Sketch" (**159-165**).
CHOOSE the person whom you either love most or admire most in your life.
REMIND yourself of the important ideas about detailed, colorful language in sections **118-122**.
MAKE two headings: "Physical Characteristics" and "Personal Characteristics."
Under each heading, LIST the finest details you can observe or remember.
CONCLUDE by writing a sentence which tells your single, strongest impression of that person. Don't settle for vague language here.

Genius Born to Humble Parents........*Writing the News Story* (6)

■ Read the chapter in *Write Source 2000* on "Writing the News Story" (**171-176**).
WRITE a brief but complete news article, with headline, which reports your own birth as a newsworthy event.
RESEARCH your news article by interviewing your parents.

Credit Where Credit Is Due ....*Citing Borrowed Works* (8)

■ Consult the "Model Works Cited Entries" chart in section **283**.
DECIDE what kind of work *Write Source 2000* is.
WRITE a correct bibliographic entry citing *Write Source 2000*.

This egg has crud on it. ....*Letter of Complaint* (7)

■ Read the guidelines for writing a letter of complaint (**214**).
   THINK of a product you've bought that doesn't work well enough or a service you've
      received that was not performed well enough.
   FIND out the address of the person who should receive your complaints.
   WRITE a letter of complaint to that person.
   PUT your letter in "Full-Block" format as described in section **204**.

Journey to the Center of the Problem .....*Personal Research* (7)

■ Read and enjoy the *Write Source 2000* tips on doing "Personal Research" (**265-270**). Pay
special attention to the four points under "Connecting: Telling Your Research Story" (**270**).
   REMEMBER a time in your life when you discovered something for yourself by tracking
      down the answer, maybe by talking to other people.
   JOT DOWN whatever you remember that fits under the four headings: 1) What I Knew,
      2) What I Wanted to Know, 3) What I Found Out, and 4) What I Learned.
   WRITE a "research story" based on your notes.

Food from the Table ....*Using Tables* (6)

■ Study the pages titled "Planet Profusion" in the Student Almanac (**809**). Pay special
attention to the table of facts about the planets.
   PICK OUT three different planets from the table.
   STUDY the facts about each one—gravity, length of year, temperature, etc.
   PRETEND you are on the planets, equipped for survival.
   WRITE an imaginative observation report telling what your experience is like on each
      of the three different planets.

My Room, No, My Bottom Drawer! .... *Prewriting: Listing* (6)

■ Survey the "Personal Writing Sampler" (**149**) and choose one type of memory to write
about.
   NOTICE the instructions for "Listing" under "Selecting a Writing Subject" (**036**).
   LIST as many thoughts and details as you can in connection with the memory you chose.
   READ your list and pull together several of the most interesting items on it.
   WRITE DOWN a *new* and *sharper* focus for your personal writing.

"Out at the Plate" ....*Titles* (7)

■ Read the comments on choosing titles in section **025**.
THINK of your entire life so far.
ASSUME that you've already written a fascinating autobiography (the story of your life). (See **133-143**.)
WRITE *five* of the best titles you can think of for your autobiography.
CHOOSE the best one and WRITE it in big letters someplace where you'll see it often.

Once Upon a Coffin ....*Short Story Sampler* (6)

■ Survey the section on "Story Writing" (**237-252**), especially the section on "A Short Story Sampler" (**247-252**).
FORM a circle with your class or a large group. (This can be fun at a party!)
SET OUT to write a horror story.
WRITE the first sentence of your story on a piece of paper as everyone else does the same.
PASS your paper to the person next to you.
WRITE a second sentence on the sheet your neighbor passes to you. *Remember:* You're trying to write a horror story. Try to catch the spirit of your partner's story and keep it up.
CONTINUE adding sentences and passing papers until your own sheet goes all around the circle and comes back to you.
DO THE SAME for a mystery, a fantasy, a science fiction story, a myth, or a fable.

Road Trip ....*Writing Dialogue* (6)

■ Read the "Guidelines for Developing Dialogue" (**255-256**).
INVENT two characters: one male, one female, one older, and one younger.
GIVE each character at least a couple of conflicting character traits (she's smart but impatient, or he's brave but depressed). Make a note of the character traits.
PUT the two characters in a car and have them talking.
WRITE three different snatches of conversation. In the first, make them *contented*. In the second, make them *upset*. In the third, make them *afraid*. (Make sure each one's distinctive character traits show through in their conversation.)

Capriccio/Mangel-wurzel/Zapateado....*Using the Dictionary* (6)

■ Thoroughly study the section on "Using the Dictionary" (**303-304**).
CHOOSE an unusual word which starts with the first two letters of your last name. Try to find a word which has a full and fairly lengthy entry in the dictionary.
READ every word and abbreviation in the dictionary entry.
WRITE an essay in which you express in full sentences and with logical organization every single piece of information you can gather from the dictionary entry.

Question Maker .... *Selecting a Writing Topic* (8)

■ Look at the "Essentials of Life Checklist" (**036**).
   CREATE *five* different topics by picking one word from each of the three columns and
      making a good question out of it: for example,
           CLOTHING   MACHINES   RULES/LAWS
   "What laws apply to the machines that manufacture clothing?"
           SENSES   PLANTS   FUEL
   "What does a log sound like when it burns?"
If any of the questions lead you to a better idea, WRITE about it.

Mind if I tape this? ...... *Interviewing/Creative Collaboration* (7)

■ Study the sections on "Interviewing" (**405-407**).
   ASK your friend to PRETEND to be someone he or she always dreamed of being. Your
      friend should try to imagine as much as possible about what that person's life is like.
   PUT ON your best interviewing behavior and interview your friend.
   WRITE out the best questions you can think of—the kind the interviewee is best prepared
      to answer and the kind that will pique other people's interest.
   BE PREPARED to go beyond your written questions as the interview develops.

Polysyllables .... *Improving Vocabulary* (8)

■ Survey the section on "Improving Vocabulary" (**371-384**); know how to use the lists of
prefixes (**374-375**), suffixes (**377**), and roots (**378-384**).
   USE the three lists to figure out the definitions of the following words:
                     philanthropy
                     prestidigitation
                     pneumoconiosis
              antidisestablishmentarianism
   CHECK your definitions against an unabridged dictionary.

"Can't See the Monkeys from the Bus" .... *Creative Thinking* (6)

■ Consult the list of "Writing Topics" (**040**) under the subheading "Describing . . . People . . .
Places . . . Things." You might want to
   READ the sections under the heading "Thinking Creatively" (**331-342**). Also
   READ the short sections on "Writing Your Own Poem" (**224-228**).
   From the list of people, places, and things, PICK one person, one place, and one thing.
      (*Hint:* Pick a *weird* combination.)
   WRITE a poem in which the *person* you chose talks about the *thing* in the *place*. (For
      example, a bus driver talks about a billboard at the zoo.)

Dear Sis, ... *Improving Reading* (8)

■ Suppose your school has assigned you to be a Big Brother or Big Sister of a younger student who is having trouble reading and remembering.
STUDY the chapter on "Study-Reading Skills" (**361-370**).
MAKE UP a name for your student.
WRITE a personal letter (see **196-202**) in which you give your student the best advice you know of for improving his or her reading.

Playing Teach ....*Understanding Essay Tests* (8)

■ Carefully study the advice on taking essay tests in section **421-427**.
GATHER together some knowledge that you recently gained in one of your non-English classes.
WRITE a good-quality essay test question to give to a student who takes that course next year.
SUBMIT your test question to the teacher of that course for a critique.

Unless what? ....*Finding a Subject* (6)

■ Read the paragraph on "Free Writing" under "Selecting a Writing Subject" (**035**).
WRITE the word "Unless" on a piece of paper and finish writing the sentence any way you can.
CONTINUE writing, going wherever your fertile mind takes you.
After 5-8 minutes, STOP and WRITE the single most important thought that has occurred to you during that time, whether you've written it yet or not.

All systems are go. .... *Taking Inventory of Your Thoughts* (7)

■ Choose a starting point for a new piece of writing using the ideas in section **034**. Especially notice the suggestions under "Personal Almanac (Inventory)" and "Life Map." Try to decide on a topic in 2-3 minutes.
USE topic number **016**, "Taking Inventory of Your Thoughts," to collect and focus your ideas.
Quickly WRITE down everything you can think of about
  1) your present **situation** as a writer,
  2) your **self** (what would this writing mean for you?),
  3) your **subject**,
  4) your **readers**,
  5) your **style** of writing (form, approach, manner, language, etc.).
CHANGE one of these five—for example, *narrow* your subject, or aim at a *different kind of reader*.
DECIDE and WRITE DOWN how the other four factors will be forced to change in view of your first change.

Have *I* Got Problems. ....*Word Problems* (6)

■ Study the "Guidelines for Solving Word Problems." Look for "Word Problems" in the index.

THINK of a situation in your own life that involves measures, distances, times, costs, weights, rates, or fractions.

WRITE up your situation in the form of a word problem (also known as a story problem).

GIVE your word problem to a neighbor in class to solve.

Croak/Cash In/Kick the Bucket.............*Using the Thesaurus* (7)

■ Read the instructions for "Using the Thesaurus" in section **302**.

CHOOSE one of the following pairs of words: find/lose, sober/drunk, build/destroy.

LOOK UP both words in a thesaurus and

STUDY the kinds of words listed under each one.

WRITE a paragraph explaining the difference you notice between the language we use for something good and for something bad.

One hand washes the other. ....*Symbols of Correction* (8)

■ See the "Symbols of Correction" on the last page of *Write Source 2000*.

EXCHANGE papers with a partner—use any paper you've written earlier and still care about.

EDIT your partner's paper, using the correction symbols wherever possible.

ADD a written comment which conveys your *personal* response to your partner's paper as a whole.

Hitting the Stacks.......................*Using the Reference Section* (6)

■ Read through the section listing reference books of special interest to young people (**298**).

SELECT a book from the list which you haven't heard of before.

GO to the library and find out how to use the book—what to look for in it, how to save time using it, etc.

WRITE a note summarizing your discoveries about the book.

GIVE the note to a neighbor in your class.

Program Planning

The information contained in the final section will help teachers plan a language program using the *Write Source 2000* handbook and the coordinating *Teacher's Guide.* Also included is a basic introduction and planning guide for the complete *Write Source 2000 Language Series,* a comprehensive language program for grades 6-8.

Building a Writing and Language Program with the *Write Source 2000* Handbook

Q. Can teachers build a language program with *Write Source 2000* and the *Teacher's Guide*?

A. Most definitely. These two resources can serve as the foundation for a contemporary language arts program promoting, among other things, student-centered language learning, writing as a process of discovery, and the reading-writing connection. These products can also serve as the foundation (and the glue) for a cross-curricular writing and learning program.

Q. How should teachers plan a program with these two resources?

A. Since *Write Source 2000* functions mainly as a writing handbook, that is where teachers should first focus their attention. Two very basic questions should be answered during initial planning: **How will writing instruction be approached?** (Will students engage in writing workshops? Will writing be integrated into thematic units?) **What types of writing will be covered?** (Will personal forms of writing be emphasized in grade 6? Will paragraphs be of primary importance in grades 6 and 7 and multi-paragraph essays in grade 8?)

"An Overview of Contemporary Writing Programs," pp. 44-52 in the *Teacher's Guide*, will help teachers answer the first question. All of the important approaches to writing instruction are discussed here. Teachers can answer the second question by reviewing the forms of writing covered in the handbook and focusing their attention on those forms that best meet the needs and nature of their students. (Teachers may also refer to the framework of writing activities for grades 6-8 listed on p. 113 in this section for a suggested sequence of writing activities.)

Q. What about the other language arts?

A. Teachers will find major sections in the handbook related to reading, thinking, and speaking and listening. Determining what concepts to cover during the course of a year is simply a matter of becoming familiar with the material.

Reading to Learn (360-387) • We suggest that a number of different study-reading strategies (KWL, mapping, . . .) be practiced at each grade level. We also suggest that the glossary of prefixes, suffixes, and roots be the focus of vocabulary study at each grade level. (Teachers should refer to "Building Vocabulary," pp. 89-90 in the *Teacher's Guide*, for additional information and ideas.)

Thinking to Learn (305-359) • This section addresses thinking from a number of different perspectives. The primary focus of attention in one grade level might be clear and logical thinking, in another grade level, creative thinking, and so on. (Teachers should refer to pp. 83-85 in the *Teacher's Guide* for additional information and ideas.)

Speaking and Listening to Learn (388-407) • The basic guidelines included in this section should be used year after year when students are involved in oral/aural work. (Teachers should refer to pp. 86-88 in the *Teacher's Guide* for additional information and ideas.)

Q. What about learning and study skills?

A. In the handbook's "Learning to Learn" section (408-457), teachers will find a variety of guidelines related to studying and learning. Perhaps writing to learn and note taking could be emphasized in one grade level, test taking in the next grade, and individual skills (setting goals, managing time, etc.) in the following grade. (Teachers should refer to pp. 76-82 in the *Teacher's Guide* for additional information and ideas related to learning.)

Q. What else should teachers remember when planning with *Write Source 2000*?

A. Teachers should always remember to turn to the "Section by Section Teacher's Notes" in the *Teacher's Guide* (pp. 11-32) whenever they are planning a unit around a particular section or chapter in the handbook. These notes provide valuable background information as well as getting-started and enrichment activities.

What specific types of writing are covered in *Write Source 2000?*

The chart below lists many of the types of writing discussed in the *Write Source 2000* handbook. The types of writing are listed in this manner to indicate a *possible* framework or sequence of activities, moving from personal writing to writing that eventually becomes more inventive and reflective. Teachers can use this framework as a starting point when planning a writing program (or individual writing activities) with the handbook.

	6	7	8
PERSONAL WRITING			
Recalling and Remembering	Writing About Experiences (144)	Writing Phase Autobiographies (133)	Writing Personal Essays (044)
	Memories of People (149)	Memories of Places (149)	Memories of Objects (149)
SUBJECT WRITING			
Introducing	Bio-Poems (158)	The Character Sketch (159)	Writing Phase Bios (151)
Describing	Descriptive Paragraphs (077) Describing a Person (068)	Descriptive Paragraphs (077) Describing a Place (069)	Describing an Object (070) Describing an Event (072)
Reporting	Writing the Basic News Story (171)	Writing the Feature Story (177)	Writing a Human Interest Story (050)
Corresponding	Writing Friendly Letters (196)	Writing Fan Letters (192)	Writing Business Letters (203)
Informing	Narrative Paragraphs (078)	Expository Paragraphs (079)	Multi-paragraph Essays (052)
Searching and Researching	Writing Summaries (184)	Writing Observation Reports (166)	Writing from an Interview (405)
	Library Report (271, 290)	Report Writing (271)	Personal Research Paper (265)
CREATIVE WRITING			
Translating	"Invented" Poetry (235)	Free-verse Poetry (224)	Traditional Poetry (233)
Inventing	Writing Fables/Myths (252)	Story Writing (237)	Patterned Stories (246)
Scripting	Dialogue Writing (253)	Monologue Writing (253, 245)	Writing Miniplays (257)
REFLECTIVE WRITING			
Analyzing	Writing a Before and After Essay (066)	Writing a Comparison and Contrast Essay (064)	Writing about Causes/Effects Problems/Solutions (066)
Persuading	Persuasive Paragraphs (080)	Writing Pet Peeves (050)	Writing Editorials (178, 074)
Reviewing	One-Paragraph Book Reviews (187)	One-Paragraph Book Reviews (187)	Multi-Paragraph Book Reviews (187)

What additional topics are covered in *Write Source 2000?*

There is an incredible amount of information covered in *Write Source 2000*, a good deal of which goes unnoticed (or unmentioned) in a quick review of the handbook's key features. What follows is a list of information teachers will discover once they carefully read through *Write Source 2000*. This list further demonstrates the handbook's potential as a teaching and learning tool.

Special Note: Refer to pages 94-110 for minilessons related to many of these writing, learning, and cross-curricular topics.

Writing-Related Topics

- Creating a Writing "SourceBank" (033-034)
- Selecting a Writing Subject (035-036)
- Writing Prompts, Topics, and Forms (039-041)
- Organizing with an Outline (059-062)
- Transition or Linking Words (089)
- Improving Your Style of Writing (116-117)
- Writing Techniques and Terms (124-128)
- Writing Fan Letters (192-195)
- Computers & Writing (287-289)
- Avoiding Fuzzy Thinking in Writing (350-355)
- Handwriting Models (911)

Language and Learning Topics

- Reading and Understanding Your Book (187)
- What Is Poetry? (221-223)
- Reading and Appreciating a Poem (229)
- An Introduction to Traditional Poetry (230-234)
- Basic Patterns for Stories (246)
- Using the Library (290-304)
- Becoming a Better Thinker (307)
- Using Your Brain (356-359)
- Word Pictures for Reading to Learn (365)
- Using Context Clues (370)
- Completing Assignments (453)
- Managing Stress (455-457)
- Improved Spelling (568-573)
- Reading Charts (811-825)

Cross-Curricular Topics in "The Student Almanac"

- Animal Facts (797)
- Braille Alphabet and Numbers (799)
- Tables of Weights and Measures (803-808)
- Planet Profusion (809)
- Periodic Table of the Elements (810)
- Improving Math Skills (843-855)
- Using the Computer (856-864)
- All About Maps (826-842)
- Historical Documents (856-888)
- Historical Time Line (889-898)

Building a Writing and Language Program with the *Write Source 2000 Language Series*

The *Write Source 2000 Language Series* is a complete language and learning program for levels 6, 7, and 8. (There is a separate program for each level.) The program provides teachers with a rich resource of activities—including, among other things, extended writing units, thematic language units, writing and language workshops, and daily language activities—plus practical guidelines for implementing and assessing student work.

▼ What is included in the series?

Each level in the *Language Series* is packaged in a program kit containing five basic elements. These elements include . . .

Write Source 2000 **Student Handbook** • A hardcover copy of the handbook is included for handy teacher reference. (Each student must have access to a copy of the handbook as well.)

Write Source 2000 Teacher's Guide • Since the *Teacher's Guide* provides so much valuable information about the handbook and language learning in general, it serves an important function in the complete program package.

Student SourceBook • Each kit includes one *Student SourceBook*, containing over 180 units and activities for teachers to reproduce and use in their classrooms. (A detailed discussion of the SourceBook activities follows on p. 117.)

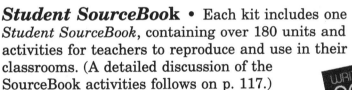

The *Program Guide* • This three-ring binder contains over 500 pages worth of information, including guidelines for program planning, daily writing and language activities, thematic units, and much more.

Classroom Posters, Wall Charts, and Bookmarks • The colorful posters and wall charts provide valuable information about reading and writing. The bookmarks list questions that will help students think and write about the books they read.

How does the *Write Source 2000 Language Series*

When **more** is less . . .

The *Write Source 2000 Language Series* actually offers more for less. Rather than a textbook which contains both instruction and activities, our program separates the two. This makes it possible for students to have access to the instructions and guidelines in the handbook for use in other classes. As we know, writing and learning don't just happen in the language classroom—they are all-school, all-day activities.

Provided below is a more detailed comparison between the *Write Source 2000 Language Series* and a traditional textbook series.

compare with a traditional textbook series?

Traditional Textbook Series		Write Source 2000 Language Series
❑ **predetermined sequence...** assumes that a writing and language program should be built around a particular series and sequence of activities located within the textbooks	■ **flexible sequence...** provides an opportunity for teachers and students to develop a language and writing sequence that truly meets their needs	
❑ **expansive text...** begins and ends with oversized texts that are seen by students as imposing and impersonal	■ **portable resource...** offers a 432-page handbook of portable information which students can refer to in the language classroom and across the curriculum	
❑ **traditional approach...** customarily addresses students in a formal tone and places a great deal of attention on isolated skills work	■ **personalized approach...** speaks in a friendly, reassuring voice that engages students in the explanations and activities	
❑ **classwide instruction...** often prescribes that certain units or chapters be taught to all students at the same time	■ **individual needs...** provides a flexible resource of activities to better meet individual teaching styles and student needs; also provides students opportunities to learn independently	
❑ **language classroom...** focuses almost exclusively on writing in the language classroom	■ **across the curriculum...** encourages writing, thinking, and learning in all content areas	
❑ **teacher centered...** is dependent on teacher instruction	■ **student centered...** encourages self-improvement and independent learning	
❑ **costly...** can be very expensive	■ **cost-effective...** is very reasonably priced	

What are the specific types of activities contained in the *Student SourceBooks?*

The activities break down in the following way (the numbers are approximate):

Extended Core Writing Units: Part I contains seven core writing units that address many of the important forms of writing covered in the handbook, including autobiographical and biographical writing, paragraphs, essays, and stories.

Writing Workshops: Part II contains many different workshop activities that will help students at all stages of the writing process, from prewriting to proofreading. Included in this section are the following sets of activities:

- 10 Prewriting Strategies
- 10 Forms of Writing
- 7 Revising Workshops
- 6 Sentence-Combining Workshops
- 10 Editing Workshops
- 7 Proofreading Workshops

Language and Learning Workshops: Part III contains language workshops that will help students better understand how words work, and learning workshops that will help them become better thinkers, study-readers, speakers, and listeners. Included in this section are the following sets of activities:

- 15 Language Workshops
- 9 Reading and Learning Strategies
- 7 Talking and Listening Activities
- 15 Thinking Workshops
- 9 Vocabulary and Word Play Activities

Minilessons: Part IV, way in the back of the book, features over 50 minilessons that relate to all of the different areas of writing, language, and learning covered in the *Write Source 2000* handbook.

What do teachers need to know about the SourceBooks?

The SourceBooks for grades 6-8 cover almost every aspect of writing and language learning. The combination of the SourceBook activities and the daily language activities in the *Program Guide* provide teachers with everything they need to plan an effective language program.

To use a SourceBook independently (rather than in conjunction with the complete program), teachers will need the *SourceBook Teacher's Edition* for their grade level. This resource contains basic planning information and an answer key.

How can teachers plan activities using the *Language Series?*

To help teachers with their planning, the *Language Series* contains a suggested yearlong timetable of activities. The timetable provides a starting point for curriculum planning. Teachers should adjust it to meet the needs of their students. (There is a separate timetable for each grade level 6, 7, and 8. There are also suggested weekly lesson plans included at each grade level.)

Special Note: The *Language Series* contains far more activities than one teacher could implement during the school year. Therefore, the timetable focuses on the core writing units and the writing and language workshops.

---

22 • LONG-RANGE PLANNING

The lessons in the suggested Yearlong Timetable for Level 6 focus primarily on key sets of writing and basic language activities in the program. Teachers should remember to adjust the timetable to meet the needs of their students or to incorporate other activities and units.

YEARLONG TIMETABLE OF LESSONS   LEVEL 6

week   topic / unit

FIRST QUARTER
1. "Getting Started" (Teacher's Guide)
2. **Writing Workshop:** Writing Process
3. **Core Writing Unit:** "Writing About Personal Experiences"
4. **Learning Workshop:** Listening, Study-Reading, or Thinking
5. **Writing Workshop:** Prewriting (Part 1)
6. **Core Writing Unit:** "Building Paragraphs: Part 1"
7. **Writing Workshop:** Sentence Errors
8. **Thematic Writing Unit:** "This is the way it happened."
9. Quarter Wrap-Up

SECOND QUARTER
10. **Language Workshop:** Nouns and Pronouns
11. **Core Writing Unit:** "Building Paragraphs: Part 2"
12/13. **Core Writing Unit:** "Writing Descriptively About People"
14. **Writing Workshop:** Proofreading (Part 1)
15. **Language Workshop:** Vocabulary

THIRD QUARTER
19. **Writing Workshop:** Reviewing Writing
20. **Writing Workshop:** Revising Writing
21. **Language Workshop:** Verbs
22. **Core Writing Unit:** "Writing Mystery Stories"
23. **Writing Workshop:** Proofreading (Part 2)
24. **Writing Workshop:** Usage
25/26. **Core Writing Unit:** "Writing a Report"
27. Quarter Wrap-Up

FOURTH QUARTER
28. **Language Workshop:** Modifiers
29. **Language Workshop:** Other Parts of Speech
30. **Core Writing Unit:** "Writing the Comparison and Contrast Essay"
31. **Writing Workshop:** Sentence Combining
32. **Writing Workshop:** Sentence Expanding
33. **Writing Workshop:** Editing for Clarity

LONG-RANGE PLANNING   23

The lessons in the suggested Yearlong Timetable for Level 7 focus primarily on key sets of writing and basic language activities in the program. Teachers should remember to adjust the timetable to meet the needs of their students or to incorporate other activities and units.

YEARLONG TIMETABLE OF LESSONS   LEVEL 7

week   topic / unit

FIRST QUARTER
1. "Getting Started" (Teacher's Guide)
2. **Core Writing Unit:** "Writing About Personal Experiences"
3. **Learning Workshop:** Reading to Learn
4. **Writing Workshop:** Prewriting (Part 1)
5. **Writing Workshop:** Sentence Errors
6. **Language Workshop:** Vocabulary
7. **Thematic Writing Unit:** "This Is Your Life!"
8. **Learning Strategies**
9. Quarter Wrap-Up or **Learning Workshop:** Listening or Thinking

SECOND QUARTER
10. **Writing Workshop:** Prewriting (Part 2)
11. **Core Writing Unit:** "Writing a Character Sketch"
12. **Writing Workshop:** Proofreading (Part 1)
13. **Language Workshop:** Nouns and Pronouns
14. **Thematic Writing Unit:** "Does It Have to Rhyme?"
15. **Writing Workshop:** Usage
16. **Core Writing Unit:** "Building Paragraphs: Part 1"
17. **Learning Strategies**
18. Semester Wrap-Up

THIRD QUARTER
19. **Core Writing Unit:** "Building Paragraphs: Part 2"
20. **Language Workshop:** Verbs
21. **Writing Workshop:** Reviewing Writing
22. **Writing Workshop:** Revising Writing
23/24. **Core Writing Unit:** "Writing a Report"
25. **Writing Workshop:** Sentence Combining
26. **Writing Workshop:** Proofreading (Part 2)
27. Quarter Wrap-Up or **Core Writing Unit:** "Writing Myths"

FOURTH QUARTER
28/29. **Core Writing Unit:** "Writing About Problems and Solutions"
30. **Writing Workshop:** Sentence Expanding
31. **Language Workshop:** Modifiers
32. **Writing Workshop:** Editing for Clarity
33. **Language Workshop:** Prepositions and Other Parts of Speech
34/35. **Thematic Writing Unit:** "I'll Ad to That!"
36. Year-End Wrap-Up

---

24   *Long-Range Planning*

The lessons in the suggested Yearlong Timetable for Level 8 focus primarily on key sets of writing and basic language activities in the program. Teachers should remember to adjust the timetable to meet the needs of their students or to incorporate other activities and units.

YEARLONG TIMETABLE OF LESSONS   LEVEL 8

week   topic / unit

FIRST QUARTER
1. "Getting Started" (Teacher's Guide)
2. **Core Writing Unit:** "Writing the Phase Autobiography"
3. **Learning Workshop:** Listening, Study-Reading, or Thinking
4. **Writing Workshop:** Prewriting (Part 1)
5. **Core Writing Unit:** "Building Paragraphs"
6. **Writing Workshop:** Sentence Errors
7/8. **Thematic Writing Unit:** "Mind if I tape this?"
9. Quarter Wrap-Up

SECOND QUARTER
10. **Writing Workshop:** Prewriting (Part 2)
11. **Core Writing Unit:** "Building Essays"
12. **Language Workshop:** Nouns and Pronouns
13. **Language Workshop:** Vocabulary
14. **Core Writing Unit:** "Writing the Phase Biography"
15. **Writing Workshop:** Proofreading (Part 1)
16. **Writing Workshop:** Usage
17. **Learning Strategies**
18. Semester Wrap-Up

THIRD QUARTER
19. **Core Writing Unit:** "Writing a Survival Story"
20. **Writing Workshop:** Reviewing Writing
21. **Writing Workshop:** Revising Writing
22. **Language Workshop:** Verbs
23/24. **Thematic Writing Unit:** "The Lively Art of Poetry"
25. **Writing Workshop:** Proofreading (Part 2)
26. **Core Writing Unit:** "Cause and Effect Writing"
27. Quarter Wrap-Up

FOURTH QUARTER
28. **Writing Workshop:** Sentence Combining or Sentence Expanding
29/30. **Core Writing Unit:** "Writing to Define"
31. **Language Workshop:** Modifiers
32. **Language Workshop:** Prepositions and Other Parts of Speech
33. **Writing Workshop:** Editing for Clarity
34/35. **Thematic Writing Unit:** "Speak Out!"
36. Year-End Wrap-Up

The Write Source Product Line

Writers Express — **A Handbook for Young Writers, Thinkers, and Learners** addresses all the different types of writing, reading, and thinking students in grades 4 and 5 do both in school and at home. This handbook provides intermediate students with the very best information related to language and learning.

Writers Express Language Series provides a writing-based language program for grades 4 and 5. (There is a separate program binder for each grade level.) Both levels coordinate with the *Writers Express* student handbook.

Writers Express SourceBooks for grades 4 and 5 contain workshop activities, minilessons, and daily proofreading sentences to help students improve their writing skills. Each SourceBook is available as a reproducible resource or in classroom sets.

Write Source 2000 — **A Guide to Writing, Thinking, & Learning** serves as the perfect student handbook for grades 6-8. It covers everything from the writing process to writing reports, from building vocabulary skills to thinking logically, from giving speeches to reading maps.

Write Source 2000 Language Series provides a writing-based language program for grades 6, 7, and 8 that is comprehensive and sequential, yet creative and flexible. (There is a separate program binder for each grade level.)

The series can serve as the focus of a new and stimulating language arts program when used with the *Write Source 2000* handbook, or it can supplement an existing program. (See page 115 for more detailed information.)

Write Source SourceBooks for grades 6, 7, and 8 contain core units, workshop activities, and minilessons—all designed to improve the students' ability to write and to learn. The SourceBooks coordinate with the complete Language Series, or they can be used separately with the *SourceBook Teacher's Editions.*

Writers INC — **A Student Handbook for Writing & Learning** reflects the best thinking on writing and learning for students in grades 9-12 and beyond. This is an all-purpose handbook and reference book for use in the English classroom and across the curriculum.

Writers INC Language Series provides the foundation for a student-centered writing and learning program for grades 9-12. (There is a separate program binder for each grade level.) Each program includes, among other things, a framework of major writing activities, a comprehensive collection of writing workshops, and a resource of daily language activities.

Writers INC SourceBooks for grades 9-12 contain bound versions of the activities in the program binders. The SourceBooks coordinate with the complete Language Series, or they can be used separately with the *SourceBook Teacher's Editions.*

Dear Parents,

I recently came across a student handbook which I think could be useful for all of our students. The handbook contains nearly everything a student needs to know about reading, writing, thinking, and studying and is an excellent reference book for both the home and school.

If you are interested in purchasing a copy for the students in your family, fill in the bottom portion of this letter and return it to me. By pooling our orders, we can get a special price. The handbooks should arrive in two to three weeks. I'm sure you'll be as impressed with the handbook as I am.

Thank you,

- -

I would like to order _____ Write Source 2000 handbook(s) at _____* each.

Total amount enclosed _____

_____

(Student's name)

*Special note to the teacher: Please call for current school prices (1-800-428-8071).

INDEX